Key Resources on Institutional Advancement

A Guide to the Field and Its Literature

A. Westley Rowland

Key Resources on Institutional Advancement

Jossey-Bass Publishers

San Francisco • London • 1986

KEY RESOURCES ON INSTITUTIONAL ADVANCEMENT
A Guide to the Field and Its Literature
by A. Westley Rowland

Copyright © 1986 by: Jossey-Bass Inc., Publishers
433 California Street
San Francisco, California 94104

&

Jossey-Bass Limited
28 Banner Street
London EC1Y 8QE

Library of Congress Cataloging-in-Publication Data

Rowland, A. Westley (date)
 Key resources on institutional advancement.

 (The Jossey-Bass higher education series)
 Includes index.
 1. Public relations—Universities and colleges—
United States—Bibliography. 2. Educational fund
raising—United States—Bibliography. 3. College
publicity—United States—Bibliography. 4. Organiza-
tional change—United States—Bibliography.
5. Communication in organizations—United States—
Bibliography. 6. College publications—United States—
Bibliography. I. Title. II. Series.
LB2342.8.R68   1986   016.6592′937873   86-10296
ISBN 1-55542-014-1

Manufactured in the United States of America

The paper in this book meets the guidelines for
permanence and durability of the Committee on
Production Guidelines for Book Longevity of the
Council on Library Resources.

JACKET DESIGN BY WILLI BAUM

FIRST EDITION

Code 8636

The Jossey-Bass
Higher Education Series

Preface

This book brings together the important literature, properly annotated, of institutional advancement. This field encompasses all the programs colleges and universities undertake to secure the resources they need to achieve their academic goals. The resources may be students, faculty, or dollars. The means of attaining them involve developing understanding and support among all of an institution's constituencies. On some campuses, the advancement function is called public affairs, college or university relations, development, or public relations. It may include programs in educational fund raising, alumni administration, institutional relations (media relations, publications and periodicals, community relations), government relations, enrollment management, and management of advancement.

The programs and activities of the Council for Advancement and Support of Education (CASE) in Washington, D.C., and its predecessor organizations have contributed to the significant body of literature that has been published on institutional advancement. This book, however, is the first to codify, organize, and annotate the extensive literature in this field.

This book will materially assist the professionalization of the advancement field. One of the most important criteria in defining a profession is the existence of a body of data, readily available, up-to-date, and usable by those who work or do research in the field. This annotated bibliography provides a compendium of that essential information for institutional advancement.

This volume is of importance to colleges and universities because it provides the materials necessary to help institutions of higher education in their fund raising, work with alumni and government, relations with the media and the community, production and dissemination of quality publications and periodicals, refinement and marketing of programs for enrollment management, use of both print and electronic media, improvement of the management of advancement, and understanding of legal issues.

Among this volume's contents are chapters on the relationship of the chief executive to advancement; advancement programs for two-year colleges, independent schools, and small and developing institutions; legal issues in advancement; and periodicals of concern to the practitioners. Its comprehensiveness will make this work a valuable resource not only to advancement professionals (estimated at more than 20,000) in our colleges and universities, but also to presidents and other senior administrators of colleges and universities, faculty who teach and do research in communication and advancement, and both general and college libraries.

The decisions as to which publications to list in this bibliography were guided by my almost forty years of experience in the field at a small denominational college and at two large multipurpose state universities. Although practical considerations prohibit every publication being listed, my goal has been to include the books and periodicals that have significantly contributed to the basic foundation of the advancement field and to its growth and development. Although all the listed publications will be helpful to the advancement practitioner, some entries are marked with a star to indicate their special value as seminal or classic works in institutional advancement.

I extend my thanks to Bonnie Jean McKenzie and Ava Shillin for their assistance with annotating and editing the entries in this book and to Sally Claydon and Carol Norris for their work in typing the manuscript.

My deep appreciation goes to the authors whose books and articles are the basis for this work. Their writing is the essential substance of this study; without their efforts, this publication would not have been possible.

My thanks go, too, to the Council for Advancement and Support of Education (CASE) for making all of its publications available to me. This was truly invaluable assistance.

Buffalo, New York   A. Westley Rowland
July 1986

Contents

11. Advancing Two-Year Colleges, Independent Schools,
    and Small, Developing Institutions   196

12. Legal Aspects of Advancement   207

13. Keeping Abreast of a Changing Field   214

    Appendix A: CASE Statement of Ethics for Advancement
    Professionals   221

    Appendix B: Periodicals, Newsletters, and Journals for
    Advancement Professionals   223

    Name Index   237

    Subject Index   247

The Author

A. Westley Rowland is professor emeritus of higher education in the Department of Educational Organization, Administration, and Policy and adjunct professor in the Department of Communication at the State University of New York at Buffalo. Previously, Rowland was vice-president for university relations at SUNY-Buffalo for fourteen years. Prior to his tenure at Buffalo, he served at Michigan State University for ten years as associate professor, university editor, executive news editor, editor of the news service, and director of the centennial celebration. The eleven previous years he spent at Alma College in Alma, Michigan, as professor and head of the speech department and director of publicity.

A native of Kalamazoo, Michigan, Rowland received his B.A. degree in social sciences in 1938 from Western Michigan University, his M.A. degree in speech from the University of Michigan in 1941, and his Ed.D. degree from Michigan State University in 1955, with higher education his major field.

Active in the field of institutional advancement for almost forty years, Rowland was president of the American College Public Relations Association (ACPRA), now the Council for the Advancement and Support of Education (CASE), in 1966–67, president of the Niagara Frontier Chapter of the Public Relations Society of America in 1968–69, and president of the State University of New York Public Relations Council in 1968–69.

From 1974 to 1976, Rowland was chair of CASE's Summer Institute in Communications. Previously, he served three years on the faculty of ACPRA's summer academy.

Rowland was awarded the Distinguished Service citation for his professional contributions to the field of institutional advancement by the State University of New York Public Relations Council in 1972. In 1978 he received the Daemen College President's Award for Outstanding Contributions to the Western New York Community; and in 1981 he was the first recipient of the Alice Beeman Award from CASE for significant editorial contributions to the field of institutional advancement. In 1983 Rowland received the Community Advisory Council's Babbidge Award for "helping to initiate, maintain and promote harmonious relations between the Western New York area and the University." He has been recognized as a Seasoned Sage of ACPRA for a quarter of a century in the profession of institutional advancement, is an accredited member of the Public Relations Society of America, and is listed in *Who's Who in America.*

Rowland is the author of *Research in Institutional Advancement,* published by CASE in 1983; general editor of the first edition (1977) and the second edition (1986) of the *Handbook of Institutional Advancement,* published by Jossey-Bass; and editor-in-chief of sixteen volumes (1978–1982) of sourcebooks on institutional advancement, published by Jossey-Bass.

Key Resources on Institutional Advancement

A Guide to the Field and Its Literature

1

An Overview of Institutional Advancement as a Professional Field

Historical Development

Institutional advancement activities in the United States began with the founding of the colonial colleges. In colonial days, as now, the greatest problem faced by college administrators was getting the money necessary to keep the colleges open, for student fees paid only a small part of the cost. Therefore, the first function of institutional advancement was fund raising.

Harvard, Yale, and William and Mary colleges had been given grants and annual subventions from their respective provincial governments by the British king. Among the newer colleges, only Dartmouth, King's, and Philadelphia were voted money from the public treasuries, and King's alone was treated generously. None ever received an annual public subsidy, despite repeated applications (McAnear, 1955, p. 24). So, in 1641, Harvard College launched the first systematic effort to raise funds by an institution on this continent, sending a trio of preachers to England on a begging mission. Once in England, these fund raisers found that they needed a fund-raising brochure—today a standard item in a fund drive—and relayed the need back to Harvard. The response to this request was *New England's First Fruits*, largely written in Massachusetts but printed in London in 1643, the first of countless billions of public relations pamphlets and brochures (Morison, 1935, p. 303).

1

Benjamin Franklin, an effective early fund raiser, offered a piece of advice still followed by professionals in the field today: "In the first place I advise you to apply to all those whom you know will give something; next, to those whom you are uncertain whether they will give anything or not, and show them the list of those who have given, and lastly, do not neglect those whom you are sure will give nothing for in some of them you will be mistaken" (Marts, 1953, p. 97). In the colonial period of 1745–1775, appeals to the general public by means of subscription lists and lotteries brought the infant colleges some funds; occasional bequests brought in a bit more. Receipts from these sources usually went to meet recurring deficits, for, as McAnear (1955) says, with the exception of King's, all the existing colleges were operating on deficit budgets.

After 1770, the raising of funds for colleges became increasingly difficult (Cutlip, 1965, p. 5). In May 1829, Mathew Carey of Philadelphia sought the interest of ninety-seven "citizens of the first respectability" to sign an appeal for funds. Carey subsequently reported: "This experiment was tried for twenty days and a half. The last four days there were but twelve dollars received and on the last day there was but a single dollar collected, which was not sufficient to pay the collector. A total of 137 subscribers giving a total of $276.50 was the net result of America's first federated fund-raising effort." One feature of Carey's imaginative, if futile, effort compares favorably with much fund raising today: the cost to carry it out was 9 percent of the amount collected, a figure Carey thought high. Whatever the results, in Carey's attempt of 1829 we find in embryo the elements of modern fund raising: the paid solicitant, the advance promotion, the classified prospect list, and the federated drive (Cutlip, 1965, p. 7).

Alumni relations as a functional program of advancement also got an early start in America. As early as 1643, former students of Harvard began returning to commencement exercises to renew acquaintance with teachers and students (Brubacher and Rudy, 1976, p. 364). At Yale, where class spirit was unusually strong, it had become the custom by 1792 for each class to appoint an alumni secretary. It was Williams College, however, that organized, in 1821, the first alumni association (Rudolph, 1962, p. 201).

Other early alumni organizations were established at Princeton University (1826), Miami University of Ohio (1832), the University of Virginia (1837), Oberlin College (1839), Denison University (1839), Brown University (1842), Amherst College (1842), Columbia University (1839), and the University of Michigan (1860). By the late nineteenth century, more than a hundred alumni organizations had been formed. The purposes of these early organizations ranged from keeping undergraduate memories fresh to keeping intellectual interests alive, from enticing student patronage to the alma mater to soliciting support funds for it (Brubacher and Rudy, 1976, p. 363).

The Association of Alumni Secretaries, the first professional organization for institutional advancement activities, was founded on February 22, 1913, at the first general conference of individuals actively engaged in alumni work in American educational institutions. About twenty-five attended the conference, which was called by H. S. Warwick, secretary of the Ohio State Association, and held at Ohio State University in Columbus. The Association of Alumnae Secretaries was founded in 1919 and the Alumni Magazines Associated in 1918; these two groups and the Association of Alumni Secretaries combined to form the American Alumni Council (AAC) at a meeting in Chapel Hill, North Carolina, in 1927, with a membership representing 249 institutions. The work of the council was carried on entirely by volunteer officers until 1951, when a central office was established in Washington, D.C.

While the first two advancement functions—fund raising and alumni relations—started very early at colleges and universities in this country, the development of others came much later. One of these, institutional (or public) relations, had its genesis in the publicity-news function. The first organization of those interested in publicity and public relations was the American Association of College News Bureaus (AACNB), founded in Chicago on April 6, 1917, at a time when there were only a few organized attempts at publicity in American colleges and universities. Although there may have been fewer than ten campuses with publicity offices prior to the end of World War I, many more campuses established news organizations shortly after the war. In the early years, publicity focused on athletic and social events, although there were some reports of faculty and administrative appointments. As other advancement functions were introduced on campuses, publications programs developed in response to their needs. Fund raisers and alumni administrators had urgent needs for periodicals and other publications to carry their messages to potential donors and to graduates of the institutions, and publications offices moved to support their activities.

To recognize the important role of publicity and news on campuses and to reflect more accurately a broader concern, the name of the AACNB was changed on April 17, 1930, to the American College Publicity Association (ACPA). From that time on, the organization matured, grew, and broadened its scope to encompass the field of public relations for higher education. Edward Bernays, pioneer public relations counsel, said in his address to the 1936 convention of the ACPA, "We should be creators of valuable newsworthy situations and events. We are not only reporters of what has happened. We are, or should be, creators of what can happen—thinkers, if you will, who can visualize the sort of projects that will strike the public fancy and will identify our colleges in the public thought." Because of the members' increased interest and involvement in educational performance, and because of the increased emphasis placed on the distinction between publicity and public relations, the name of the organization was changed to the American College Public Relations Association (ACPRA) at its 1946 convention. A national office was established in Washington, D.C., on October 1, 1950. Government relations, an emerging area of great importance to colleges and universities, got its start as a formal program with ACPRA conferences on the topic in 1963 and 1967. An ACPRA staff member appointed in 1973 was later given the new title of vice-president for government relations, reflecting the importance of this function.

Many colleges and universities eventually had memberships in both the American Alumni Council and the American College Public Relations Association. As they grew, the two organizations began to overlap and duplicate each other's services in such areas as fund raising, administration, and publications, while educational institutions were paying dues to both. Therefore, after more than a decade of active discussions, the AAC and the ACPRA merged to form a new organization, the Council for Advancement and Support of Education (CASE), on May 28, 1974. Alice Beeman, for five years the chief executive of the American Association of University Women, was named CASE's first president, and Edwin M. Crawford, vice-president for public affairs at the University of Virginia, became chairperson of the Organizing Board.

In July 1984, when CASE commemorated its tenth anniversary at its national assembly in Chicago, it had 2,500 institutional members (it now has more than 2,750) and approximately 7,500 individual members. James L. Fisher, who had become CASE's second president in 1978, summarized some of the organization's achievements in 1983–84 and compared them to the 1982–83 year: eighty-four conferences (more than four times as many as in the previous year); a total attendance of 11,200 in district and national conferences (twice as much participation as in the previous year); one and a half times as many publications and more than seven times as much grant support as in 1982–83.

Enrollment management is one of the areas in which CASE has been active. Although advancement practitioners and student recruitment staff at some colleges and universities had worked cooperatively for many years, enrollment management (more narrowly conceived as student recruitment) developed as a program area of advancement in the early 1970s. CASE and the College Entrance Examination Board cosponsored conferences in recruitment communications in 1973 and 1974; CASE devoted the February 1976 issue of its journal, *CASE Currents,* to the topic of recruitment and in 1979 published the book *A Marketing Approach to Student Recruitment.*

To help attract public attention to higher education, CASE has sponsored a "Mindpower Campaign," a "Professor of the Year" competition, and National Higher Education Week. It cosponsored the first full-scale national survey on public attitudes toward higher education in 1982 and 1983. It has also established a National Clearinghouse for Corporate Matching Gift Information and publishes an annual directory of government programs

(CASE Handbook of Federal Relations) to help member institutions take advantage of available grants and to encourage them to be more effective in influencing policy, as well as being a driving force in the Action Committee for Higher Education (ACHE), a coalition of educational associations that has been highly effective in alerting the public to the effects on education of proposed federal budget cuts. *CASE Currents* and the organization's other publications and programs have won more than forty national awards from other organizations. Finally, in cooperation with the American Council on Education and the Association of Governing Boards of Universities and Colleges, CASE has initiated a three-year program to enhance unity among all segments of higher education.

The Role of Institutional Advancement
in Colleges and Universities

Institutional advancement is as vital and as essential as any other major function of a college or university (academics, business, research, student affairs, or health sciences)—in fact, in the long run, it makes possible the maximum achievement of all other functions of an institution. Without a broad, effective program of institutional advancement, no college or university can hope to gain wide support or to attract sufficient resources from all its constituencies to allow it to achieve its educational goals.

The mission of institutional advancement is to provide effective channels of communication among administration, faculty, students, and staff and between these groups and the many external publics of the institution. Thus, institutional advancement is responsible for developing understanding and support for all the institution's programs and activities. To carry out this function, institutional advancement melds together the functions of institutional relations, information services, educational fund raising, alumni administration, publications, and government relations, all under the direction of the manager of the advancement function. Its success depends on a close integration of a group of well-qualified professionals functioning in such diverse areas as writing, editing, printing, designing, planning, speaking, and, most important of all, interpersonal relations with a multitude of individuals and groups, both within the college or university and in the outside community.

The task of interpretation, of developing understanding and goodwill, and of maintaining effective institutional relations for a college or university is demanding and never completed. Its challenge is to meet new demands, to counter unfair and inaccurate criticism, and to adjust to new conditions with creative solutions. The extent to which society will support an institution of higher education is determined over the long run by how people feel about the institution—how well they understand its mission, to what extent they feel that it contributes to their total welfare, and, ultimately, how deeply they are willing to dig into their pocketbooks to support it. It is the responsibility of institutional advancement to create a climate of public support for a college or university; in the final analysis, institutional advancement makes an institution possible.

PRINCIPLES OF ADVANCEMENT

Since advancement's beginnings in the early 1900s, certain principles have evolved in the field, the result of the maturing of the area as a profession and the extensive work in professional development carried on by the Council for Advancement and Support of Education and its predecessor organizations. These principles are discussed here to assist advancement practitioners as they work to improve their roles in the colleges and universities of the nation.

Institutional advancement must clearly establish its goals and determine how effective they are in supporting institutional goals. The raison d'être and viability of the advancement function rest on its ability to secure understanding and support for the goals of a college or university from all its publics. There is no greater principle than this. Basic and preliminary to any attempt at goal implementation are a clearly written statement of the mission and goals of the institution and an equally definitive statement of how institutional advancement programs can assist in meeting these institutional goals. The real problem comes in effectively meshing activities directed toward these goals and in developing a finely calibrated method for evaluating the degree of success that institutional advancement programs have attained in meeting them.

Presidents of colleges and universities cannot devote their attention to the details of effective news releases, a cleverly designed view book, a smoothly operated dedication ceremony, the number of speaking engagements arranged by the speakers' bureau, general plans for an annual fund campaign, or even a meeting of legislators on campus. Although such matters are important, to the president and the board of trustees, the "bottom line," the ultimate outcome, is how effectively the institutional advancement program has helped the institution to meet its goals and solve its problems. We all realize the impossibility of hitting a target when we do not know where the target is and recognize the truth of the insight, as old as the Greeks, that no wind is favorable to a person who does not know to what port he or she is sailing. Thus, the coalescing of institutional mission and institutional advancement goals is fundamental and of the highest priority.

Institutional advancement is an institutional commitment. It is not the exclusive concern of a small group of professionals in the college or university advancement offices; rather, it is a total concept, one in which the entire institution is involved and has a crucial stake. Institutional advancement is a way of life, not a bag of tricks or a bundle of techniques.

Practically everything that happens at or to a college or university makes some contribution toward its reputation and its image, good or bad. Each action, each program, each policy, and each performance become part of the institution's total institutional advancement program. One of the most important places where institutional advancement occurs is the classroom. Here, where instruction takes place, most institutions make major contributions to their reputations and to their advancement programs. How students feel about the teaching effectiveness of the faculty is vital, for this is what the students discuss with their friends, with their fellow students, with prospective students, with their parents, and with their neighbors back in their hometowns. Hence, the instructional link, the academic character of the teaching, becomes an indispensable ingredient in the total institutional advancement program. The research programs of major colleges and universities are another essential element in the institutional advancement program. The reputations of many of the major institutions of this country in research accomplishments have significantly affected how people feel about them, what grants they receive from government, foundations, and corporations, and the nature of the faculty and staff who are attracted to them.

The relationship of a college or university to its immediate community—how the institution is viewed as a citizen of that community—is fundamental to its image. If the institution's facilities are made available to community groups, if programs are mounted that are of interest to the broader community, if an effective speakers' bureau provides good programs for community groups, if community citizens are involved in advisory councils and search committees, then the possibilities for effective advancement programs are immeasurably increased. But institutional advancement is even more than this. How custodians treat visitors, how secretaries answer telephones and respond to questions, the participation of faculty members in community activities and concerns, and the institution's support of charitable programs—all these are examples of ways the advancement program is implemented. The speeches made by college or university personnel, especially the president, the courteous security officer, the clarity of the admissions policies, and the quality of dormitory life and food services are part of the multitude of functions making up an effective institutional advancement program. In reality, colleges and universities do not have a choice as to whether they are going to have an institutional advancement program. Such programs are inherently built into every institution; the only choice is whether those programs are effective.

There is no miracle method or silver-bullet technique for securing good institutional relations. Effectiveness over the long run consists of carefully delineated objectives and a program for effectively meeting them. Success will be determined by how effectively the professional staff and others in the institution can work together to produce a total advancement program. Effective institutional relations is not something that can be established once and then automatically kept for all time; it must be worked at continuously. It is important to note that every institution has an image built up in the minds of its publics; the only question is whether that image is a good one or a bad one. An institutional advancement program is a race that every institution must run, and the nature of that program will determine the success of a college or university. The advancement program will not and cannot be any more effective than the institution. Strengths must be identified and weaknesses recognized and corrected. There are no communication techniques, no matter how effective, that by themselves can make a poor institution into one of quality and excellence.

Institutional advancement officers must be concerned with changing with—and as fast as—the times. Like it or not, we cannot cling forever to what Thomas Wolfe has called "the old forms and systems of things which seemed everlasting but are changing all the time." The last twenty years have hammered home with ever-quickening blows the fact that change is to be a permanent feature of our environment—probably its most characteristic feature—and its pace will continue to increase in the years ahead. The only thing we know for certain is that what we do today will be done differently tomorrow.

All of us have experienced changes in where we live, how we live, and how much we live on, and who our neighbors are. Our government has changed. Our relationships to the outside world have altered. Our pastimes are not the same. Our expectations have been transformed. Nothing has changed so much as our institutions themselves—their services, interests, numbers, enrollments, staffs, budgets, and future aspirations. The entire framework and pattern of higher education have been transformed. There is a managerial revolution going on in higher education, and institutional advancement officers must be a part of it. We cannot afford to repeat the past—to do things the same way we did them ten, fifteen, or twenty years ago. Knowledge is doubling every eight to ten years or faster, and, if we are not careful, we run the risk of becoming obsolete.

How do we avoid the fate of the dinosaur? We must embrace and become masters of the new technology; we must constantly renew and update our skills; we must read more, absorb more, think more, and do more. As the Red Queen in *Through the Looking Glass* tells us, "It takes all the running you can do to keep in the same place. If you want to get somewhere else, you must run at least twice as fast as that." Somehow, institutional advancement officers must find ways to run faster.

Colleges and universities will have to change—a new clientele will have to be sought, new priorities established, new economies practiced. Although institutional advancement officers are already coping with these problems, they will be challenged to do more, to do it better, and to do it with less. Obviously, to be innovative and "run twice as fast," institutional advancement officers will be compelled to reduce, curtail, or totally eliminate something they are doing now if they want to do something new.

There must be a special operational relationship between the president of an institution and the manager of the advancement program. Because the president is, by virtue of his or her position, the college's chief institutional advancement officer, it follows that a special functional relationship must exist between the president and the institutional advancement officers. As chief executive of the institution, the president reflects the goals and objectives of the college or university and, in fact, plays a major role in defining them. In addition, he or she is the major interface with all of the institution's various publics. For these reasons, it is imperative that the institutional advancement officers work closely and in concert with the president on all institutional advancement programs if they are to be effective.

The goals and objectives of the president and the institutional advancement officers are those of the institution. This unity of purpose demands a unique and closer relationship than do the functions of other divisions within the institution. For those readers who find this last statement pretentious or exaggerated, I propose the following for their consideration: unlike departments that function more or less independently, the institutional advancement division must be intimately familiar with every major aspect of that institution. In addition to the institution's

organizational structure, the advancement officers must be equally
familiar with the history of the institution, with its policies and
programs, with its strengths and weaknesses, and, obviously, with
its goals and objectives. Consequently, such officers should be
regularly informed of all major policy decisions and changes; they
should be kept abreast of possible organizational changes within
the institution and any other developments that are vital in the
relationship of the institution to its many publics. "Briefing"
sessions for institutional advancement personnel can occur only
with presidential sanction and cooperation.

The president's stand in matters of budget necessarily
affects the functioning and even the existence of the institutional
advancement division. To be viable, this division must be allotted
an operating budget that is commensurate with the institution's
commitment to advancement. So central is the role of the president
to the success or failure of an institutional advancement program
that his or her lack of participation and support can negate any
efforts made in this direction.

Another important consideration in defining the role of
the president is the proper utilization of the institutional advancement personnel. Some presidents have not used institutional
advancement personnel with maximum effectiveness. The managers of institutional advancement programs and personnel in
institutional relations, fund raising, alumni relations, government
relations, and publications and periodicals have great potential to
make the life of the president easier and the programs of the
institution more effective.

*Institutional advancement officers, since they are among
the few administrators of a college who can truly see the institution as a whole, have an integrative role.* By the nature of their
function, they have a broad overview of the whole institution: its
history, its goals and objectives, its faculty, students, and staff, and
its problems. They cannot be narrow specialists. In a sense, they
must be expert in all areas of teaching, research, and public
service, because they are charged with responsibility for interpreting the whole institution to all its publics and securing support
from them. Because of the work of advancement officers, the
academic program will be more effective, the research activities

better understood, and the public service program more relevant to the community. Their efforts maximize all functions of colleges and universities.

Because this integrative function exists, the institutional advancement officer not only must have a deep concern for and understanding of his or her own institution but must stand as a surrogate for all of higher education. The advancement professional must have extensive knowledge of such crucial issues as institutional finance and declining resources, enrollment projections, collective bargaining and unions, affirmative action and equal opportunity programs, specialized programs for the disadvantaged, forms of governance, innovative academic programs, productivity and accountability of faculty, recurrent education, statewide coordination, problems of the commuter student, the scope of international education, and the need for higher education to participate in resolving such societal problems as poverty, substandard housing, pollution, inadequate transportation, and the lack of ethics in government. The integrative role of institutional advancement officers gives them unusual opportunities to serve their institutions.

Institutional advancement officers must carry out their functions as professional communicators and interpreters of the colleges of the nation with openness and candor and at the highest ethical level. All practitioners of the profession of institutional advancement face the challenge of effectively interpreting their campuses to the larger external community. How can they best describe and explain to taxpayers, parents, legislators, trustees, donors, churches, and alumni such matters as the demand for divestiture of investments by colleges and universities in corporations doing business in South Africa, the declining economic support for colleges and universities, the demand for accountability, the activities of a faculty member, protection of academic freedom, unionism and collective bargaining, affirmative action and equal opportunity, faculty strikes, student behavior and dress, coed housing, the sale of liquor on campus, and the departure of in loco parentis? To carry out this heavy responsibility and maintain credibility requires skill, frankness, good judgment, and honesty.

The institutional advancement officer must be concerned with being an educator first and with being a professional institutional advancement officer second. An advancement practitioner who hopes for acceptance in the academic community must first be an educational scholar in his or her own right to achieve this kinship. Questions that need to be answered are: How are institutional advancement officers conceived by academic colleagues? Are they, in fact, colleagues? Are they part of the central core of higher education, or are they on the periphery? It seems obvious that, if institutional advancement officers are to successfully carry out the important role assigned to them, if they are to be an integral part of the academy they seek to advance and support, then the individual concerns of management, development, institutional relations, alumni relations, government relations, and publications must be merged into the primary role of educators. This means securing advanced degrees, holding a deep respect for the academic, having a high sense of honesty and integrity, respecting confidences, and having a commitment to research, public service, and writing. Education, more than anything else, is the institutional advancement officer's business, and no amount of skill or techniques can substitute for this basic concept.

Institutional advancement officers must continue to be concerned about professionalization. It should be noted that this statement does not ask whether institutional advancement is a profession in the sense that medicine, dentistry, and law are professions; it is directed more toward the question of what is being done now and what should be done in the future to move the institutional advancement person toward being more professional. Some feel that this is not even an important question—that if the job is done well and the goals and objectives of institutional advancement are met, there will be no concern about whether the individual is a professional. However, many—perhaps most—practicing institutional advancement officers are concerned about professionalization, what is involved in becoming more professional and how one goes about it.

Some people in the field would have it attempt to become a profession like law or medicine; others reject such an idea. But what kind of standards should institutional advancement have? At the present time, the basic criterion for entering the field is whether one can get a job. It is true that many advancement officers have come from a background of journalism, but there are also many today whose backgrounds are in teaching, business, and other areas. The key questions are: What qualifications are necessary to become an institutional advancement officer? Can standards, educational and otherwise, for entering the field be developed? Does an identifiable theory, a body of knowledge, underlie advancement work? Can a grasp of this knowledge and theory be measured? Is there a way to predict success in the practice of institutional advancement activities? Can we demand adherence to a code of ethics? The Public Relations Society of America (PRSA) in 1965 instituted a program whereby its members might become accredited by passing a written examination supervised by a professional testing organization and an oral examination conducted by a three-person team. Since 1969, accreditation has been required for eligibility for active membership. The purpose is to help raise professional standards and improve the practice of public relations by giving special recognition to those members of PRSA who have demonstrated a high level of competence and fitness for the profession. Is this procedure meaningful? Does it have any implications for institutional advancement officers?

A much better job must be done of developing educational programs for those who wish to enter the field. This means closer collaboration with colleges and universities in the development of broad-based, interdisciplinary degree programs and internships, special work with high school and college counselors, and special publications to explain the nature of advancement work, its advantages, disadvantages, and challenges. The future of the field of institutional advancement is directly related to the quality of young people who can be recruited. The Council for Advancement and Support of Education has a varied program of institutes and workshops for the continuing education of its members. Certainly, programs for newcomers to the field of institutional advancement, as well as activities addressed to those in midcareer and the long-time professional, are important responsibilities of CASE. Its annual national assembly and district conferences will continue to serve as a means to keep the membership informed and up to date.

The institutional advancement manager must function at the highest policy level. He or she should be a member of the president's cabinet, have ready access to all institutional personnel and policies, and report directly to the president. The manager of advancement should feel that the president's door is always open to him or her, especially in times of conflict and emergency. The advancement function is most effective when authority is centralized in a manager who functions at the level of a vice-presidency or its equivalent.

Evaluation is essential to effective institutional advancement. Continuing feedback and information from all of an institution's constituencies are the raw materials for change, correction, and redirection. The advancement team must listen closely to what the publics of a college or university have to say.

References

Brubacher, J. S., and Rudy, W. *Higher Education in Transition.* (3rd ed.) New York: Harper & Row, 1976.

Cutlip, S. M. *Fund Raising in the United States.* New Brunswick, N.J.: Rutgers University Press, 1965.

McAnear, B. "College Founding in American Colonies, 1745-1775." *Mississippi Valley Historical Review,* 1955, *52,* 24-44.

Marts, A. C. *Philanthropy's Role in Civilization.* New York: Harper & Row, 1953.

Morison, S. E. *The Founding of Harvard College.* Cambridge, Mass.: Harvard University Press, 1935.

Rudolph, F. *The American College and University.* New York: Random House, 1962.

2

Fundamental Resources for Advancement Professionals

As a relatively new and growing field, institutional advancement is essentially a confederation of diverse disciplines. This chapter annotates publications that serve as an integrating element in advancement, dealing with general topics that cut across functions and have implications for several programs in the advancement field. Because institutional advancement officers are involved in interpreting not only their own institutions but higher education in general, their work requires a broad understanding of higher education itself—its history, its purpose, and its problems— and a deep respect for the learning process. To assist advancement professionals in acquiring this understanding, the chapter begins with a discussion of publications that serve as foundation works in higher education.

The next section of the chapter deals with career preparation and the development of advancement professionals. The publications annotated in this section present ideas for advancing one's career in the profession and analyze current practices and pay scales in the field. Topics range from working with consultants to a report on the Greenbrier Conference, which laid the groundwork for modern advancement practice.

The final section of the chapter annotates general works in the field of advancement. It begins with a discussion of a general advancement publication of major importance to the advancement professional: the *Handbook of Institutional Advancement* (entry number 54; the major parts of the *Handbook* are annotated in appropriate sections throughout this book.) The remainder of this final section of the chapter covers the use of volunteers; the role of trustees in advancement; research and evaluation; marketing; and the use of computers in advancement.

Volunteers work in many areas of advancement, especially alumni relations and fund raising. The publications annotated here were chosen to assist the advancement practitioner in using volunteers more effectively. Because trustees play a key role in advancing, interpreting, and securing support for colleges and universities, and because many advancement professionals must work with trustees and their committees, publications relating to trustees' role in advancement are also discussed here.

Surveying college and university publics is part of the overall communication process that is vital to the mission of the advancement program. The various constituencies of a college or university must feel that they are an integral part of the institution if they are to support its mission, goals, and objectives. Publications are presented here that assist the advancement professional in gathering information about how the institution is perceived by its constituencies, both external (alumni, media, government officials, parents, accrediting agencies, prospective donors, and the general public) and internal (faculty, students, and staff), and in choosing marketing strategies to present those constituencies with a positive picture of the institution. Current emphasis on accountability and the need to justify a program's existence make research a high priority for the advancement professional. Research, evaluation, and marketing studies can provide valuable data for decision making, can uncover new, more effective ways of doing things, and can validate (or invalidate) an advancement program's usefulness.

Foundation Works in Higher Education

General Administration

1   American Council on Education. *1984–1985 Fact Book on Higher Education.* New York: Macmillan, 1985. 199 pages.

This important source for higher education data provides easy access to a wide range of vital information. It covers the six major subject areas of faculty and staff, earned degrees, students, enrollments, institutions, and demographic/economic data. This is an annual publication.

2   Balderston, Frederick E. *Managing Today's University.* San Francisco: Jossey-Bass, 1974. 307 pages.

This work suggests a variety of ideas on how universities can identify and measure the components of complex organizations as they seek to become more accountable. Major topics include management as process, reasons why management has become an important issue, values that condition and motivate behavior of persons in the university, the structural frame of the university's constituencies, the need for policy analyses, market indicators, cost analysis, and resources and budgets.

3   Carnegie Commission on Higher Education. *Priorities for Action: Final Report.* New York: McGraw-Hill, 1973. 167 pages.

Established in 1967, the commission has issued twenty-one special reports on its many years of study. The topics selected for analysis in this final report are clarification of purposes, preservation and enhancement of quality and diversity, advancement of social justice, more effective governance, and more effective use of resources.

4 Carnegie Council on Policy Studies in Higher Education. *Three Thousand Futures: The Next Twenty Years for Higher Education.* San Francisco: Jossey-Bass, 1980. 439 pages.

In this last of a series of topical reports issued by the Carnegie Council on Policy Studies in Higher Education, the authors take a close look at the direction of higher education for the next twenty years. They examine both the hopes and the fears of educational leaders and analyze the probability of their being realized. The book takes a critical look at enrollment projects and forms of support and recommend possible courses of action, including a more extensive use of private funds to support higher education.

★5 Keller, George. *Academic Strategy: The Management Revolution in American Higher Education.* Baltimore, Md.: Johns Hopkins University Press, 1983. 211 pages.

Part 1 of this description of the management revolution taking place in the administration of higher education depicts the nature of the revolution, describes the new management approaches being tried, and reviews the state of planning theory and practice. Part 2 provides an explanation of strategic planning and makes recommendations for introducing these methods into campus decision-making processes. Keller believes that strategic planning, coupled with "thoughtfully constructed alterations" in governance, will assist institutions in becoming more effective and more efficient.

6 Rourke, Francis E., and Brooks, Glenn E. *The Managerial Revolution in Higher Education.* Baltimore, Md.: Johns Hopkins University Press, 1966. 184 pages.

This study examines the internal rationalization process that has taken place within colleges and universities. The managerial revolution is defined as the increasing tendency toward automation, the use of data gathering and research as a basis for policy formulation, and the development of objective criteria for making resource-allocation decisions. The authors discuss the impact on higher education of this revolution, which they consider a breaking point from the traditionally unstructured and more casual methods used in the past.

7   Stauffer, Thomas (ed.). *Beyond the Falling Sky: Surmounting Pressures on Higher Education.* Riverside, N.J.: Macmillan, 1981. 208 pages.

This work offers practical solutions for finding (and keeping) administrative talent, increasing productivity and opportunity, and effectively dealing with many other crises of the 1980s.

8   Tate, Pamela J., and Kressel, Marilyn (eds.). *The Expanding Role of Telecommunications in Higher Education.* New Directions for Higher Education, no. 44. San Francisco: Jossey-Bass, 1983. 115 pages.

This sourcebook explores the growing educational, financial, and legal impact of telecommunications technology on higher education. Focusing specifically on the areas of administration, program development, instruction, and public service, the authors examine some of the questions these technologies raise with respect to copyrights, licensure, funding, accreditation, student financial aid, and other regulatory and policy issues.

9   Tinsley, Adrian, Secor, Cynthia, and Kaplan, Sheila (eds.). *Women in Higher Education Administration.* New Directions for Higher Education, no. 45. San Francisco: Jossey-Bass, 1984. 96 pages.

This work investigates how women typically advance in higher education administration, what personal and institutional obstacles can impede their advancement, and how women can acquire the leadership skills essential to success in top administrative positions. It provides suggestions on how institutions can actively recruit and advance women administrators, describing a formal development process and detailing successful programs that have helped women increase expertise in such areas as planning and budgeting. It includes a discussion of increasing networks, mentoring, and other activities that are critical to professional development.

Economics of Higher Education

★**10**   Bowen, Howard R. *Investment in Learning: The Individual and Social Value of American Higher Education*. San Francisco: Jossey-Bass, 1977. 507 pages.

To achieve his purpose of building "a bridge linking the world of higher educational research to the world of higher educational policy," Bowen utilizes information from studies in many fields to consider outcomes of higher education. But this is not simply a compendium, as he interprets, evaluates, raises methodological questions, and attempts to provide analysis where data are weak. He ultimately compares the outcomes and the costs and suggests policy conclusions.

11   Bowen, Howard R., and Servelle, Paul. *Who Benefits from Higher Education and Who Should Pay?* Washington, D.C.: American Association for Higher Education, 1972. 49 pages.

This work, which examines the issue of who benefits from and who should pay for higher education, is based on the idea that the allocation of costs between students and society should be related to the benefits—social and individual—resulting from higher education.

12   Cooke, Alfred L. (ed.). *Planning Rational Retrenchment*. New Directions for Institutional Research, no. 24. San Francisco: Jossey-Bass, 1979. 97 pages.

This volume emphasizes techniques that institutional researchers and planners have used to provide administrative support in the decision-making process during times of retrenchment. Included are discussions on the use of the systems concept, the use of cooperation between institutions for the provision of institutional research services, integrated planning, and use of faculty productivity as a mechanism for faculty retrenchment.

13   Levine, Arthur, Green, Janice, and Associates. *Opportunity in Adversity: How Colleges Succeed in Hard Times.* San Francisco: Jossey-Bass, 1985. 317 pages.

The authors provide an excellent analysis of the opportunities open to postsecondary institutions that are prepared to respond to today's social and economic pressures. The book describes how five college leaders transformed troubled institutions into models of collegiate success and examines in detail the priorities that are critical to institutional success in hard times, including commitment to strong leadership, to faculty development, and to effective programs of student recruitment and resource management. Advancement practitioners will find of special interest the chapters "A Historical Look at Institutional Success in Hard Times," by Frederick Rudolph and "Leadership: Golden Rules of Practice," by Leon Botstein.

Higher Education and Society

★**14**   Altbach, Philip G., and Berdahl, Robert O. *Higher Education in American Society.* Buffalo, N.Y.: Prometheus Books, 1981. 326 pages.

This book focuses on the key question of how institutions of higher education can best prepare themselves for assimilation into the mainstream of society. Social, political, and economic changes have brought this question to the forefront, and the wide-ranging impact of these forces on higher education is addressed within the board context of autonomy and accountability. The authors have divided the book into three sections. The first elaborates on such fundamental topics as the historical background to the current scene, the origin and evolution of academic freedom in the United States, and recent developments concerning academic freedom and includes an essay on the broad concepts of accountability and autonomy. Part 2 covers in detail the major external constituencies of universities and colleges. The third part presents analyses of the reactions of the major internal constituencies to the increased roles of external forces. The advancement officer will find this a valuable book.

15   Birnbaum, Robert. *Maintaining Diversity in Higher Education.* San Francisco: Jossey-Bass, 1983. 209 pages.

This book describes and analyzes how colleges and universities differ regarding program structure, administrative systems, student body composition, values, and other variables. It details the purposes and functions of diversity in higher education and discusses its value to society. It considers whether diversity has been decreasing as institutions strive to cope with society's demands, economic pressure, and increased public control and recommends ways to enhance and protect diversity in higher education, allowing for continued responsiveness to the needs of its various constituents.

16   Bok, Derek. *Beyond the Ivory Tower: Social Responsibilities of the Modern University.* Cambridge, Mass.: Harvard University Press, 1982. 318 pages.

Through examination of the university's many ethical and social responsibilities, this book moves from a consideration of basic academic values to a discussion of proposals for making use of the university's academic resources to better address such problems as racial inequality, the decline of ethical standards, the need for technological innovation, and the desire for economic development in the Third World. In the last section, Bok, who is president of Harvard University, suggests that the university attack social injustice through such nonacademic means as taking formal stances on political issues and boycotting companies.

17   Perkins, James A. *University as an Organization.* New York: McGraw-Hill, 1972. 273 pages.

This work is a collection of very useful papers that delineate the distinctive character of academic organizations, considered both in themselves and with reference to nonacademic enterprises.

18   Robinson, George M., and Moulton, Janice. *Ethical Problems in Higher Education*. Englewood Cliffs, N.J.: Prentice-Hall, 1985. 112 pages.

This book provides a clear and simple introduction to basic ethical theory and describes the moral problems that are crucial in the day-to-day operation and long-term planning of colleges and universities. Considering the viewpoints of students, legislators, faculty, administrators, and funding agencies, the authors address such ethical problems as academic freedom, research fraud, tenure and promotion, plagiarism, fairness in admissions, and teacher ethics.

★**19**   Stadtman, Verne E. *Academic Adaptations: Higher Education Prepares for the 1980s and 1990s*. San Francisco: Jossey-Bass, 1980. 207 pages.

This report, prepared for the Carnegie Council on Policy Studies in Higher Education, reviews the current status and future possibilities of higher education. The study is based upon surveys of college and university presidents, student affairs officers, and other administrators concerned with finance and academic programs. Beginning with an examination of the people in higher education—students, faculty, presidents, and trustees—it then takes an institutional focus, examining changes in diversity in higher education, adaptations to decreasing enrollments, and other issues. The author found increased quality to be the first priority and financing the major issue for consideration in the 1980s and 1990s. He recommends nine strategies for the future, including analyses of future enrollments, planning methods, and means for strengthening administrative leadership.

History of Higher Education

20   "American Higher Education: Toward an Uncertain Future." *Daedalus*, 1974, *103* (entire issue 4) and 1975, *104* (entire issue 1).

These two volumes of *Daedalus* present over eighty articles on the future of higher education in America. The first deals with primarily internal issues: the purposes and goals of higher education, liberal versus professional education, curricular and institutional problems and reforms, minorities in higher education, and educational ethics, values, and beliefs. The second deals with primarily external issues: academic freedom, autonomy, accountability, education's relation to local, state, and federal government, to the general public, and to private industry.

21 Barzun, Jacques. *The American University: How It Runs, Where It Is Going.* New York: Harper & Row, 1968. 319 pages.

This exposition examines how the university works, what is crucial to quality in American higher education, what dangers threaten it, and how the university relates to the world. Barzun argues that, rather than a single-minded, easily defined American university, there now is a "big corporation" that does not always understand why it is doing what it is doing.

★22 Brubacher, John S., and Rudy, Willis. *Higher Education in Transition.* (3rd ed.) New York: Harper & Row, 1976. 546 pages.

This book constitutes a basic, general history of American higher education, beginning with a description of early colonial colleges and ending with a discussion of "Distinguishing Features of American Higher Education." Other chapters that advancement practitioners will find to be of special interest are "The Federal Government and Higher Education," "The Philosophy of Higher Education," "Academic Freedom," and "Enlarging Scope of the Administration of Higher Education."

23 Jencks, Christopher, and Riesman, David. *The Academic Revolution.* Garden City, N.Y.: Doubleday, 1968. 580 pages.

This sociological and historical analysis of American higher education begins with a general theory about the development of

American colleges and universities and then discusses the different types of institutions and their relationship to the various interest groups that founded them. It describes and evaluates the past and speculates on the future of these relationships.

★**24** Kerr, Clark. *Uses of the University.* (3rd ed.) Cambridge, Mass.: Harvard University Press, 1982. 204 pages.

This volume is based on the 1963 Godkin Lectures delivered at Harvard University by Kerr, who was then president of the University of California. In his lectures, Kerr provides an analysis of the significant developments of American higher education and the role of the university in contemporary society. This role, according to the author, "is reshaping the very nature and quality of the university. . . . A vast transformation that has taken place without a revolution." This transformation he identifies as the "multiversity," a city of infinite variety. The rest of the book is devoted to an analysis of the forces at work in that transformative process.

25 Metzger, Walter (ed.). *Dimensions of Academic Freedom.* Urbana: University of Illinois Press, 1969. 121 pages.

This book offers four good essays, with Walter Metzger and Arthur DeBardeleben in particular offering excellent analyses of academic freedom.

26 Newman, John Henry. *Idea of a University.* Garden City, N.Y.: Image Books, 1959. 428 pages.

This important collection of essays provides a useful analysis of university education in the nineteenth century, as well as a discussion of knowledge as an end in itself. Despite its date of publication, the issues presented are still relevant today.

★**27** Rudolph, Fredrick. *American College and University: A History.* New York: Random House, 1965. 516 pages.

This basic general history of American higher education from colonial times to the twentieth century is required reading for the advancement officer who needs to become acquainted with the history of higher education in the United States. The work begins with the colonial college and ends with the American consensus. Included are discussions of the extracurriculum and the rise of football, financing of the colleges, the elective principle, and the education of women.

★28   Veysey, Laurence. *Emergence of the American University.* Chicago: University of Chicago Press, 1965. 505 pages.

A detailed study of the "revolution" in American higher education between 1870 and World War I, this work examines how the four themes of utility, discipline and piety, research, and liberal culture have influenced the development of the modern university.

Organization and Governance

29   Baldridge, J. Victor, Curtis, David V., Ecker, George, and Riley, Gary L. *Policy Making and Effective Leadership: A National Study of Academic Management.* San Francisco: Jossey-Bass, 1978. 290 pages.

This volume provides a comparative analysis of college and university governance and of organizational features that affect decision making and professional practice. Based on information from hundreds of campuses and thousands of campus administrators and faculty members, as well as detailed institutional case studies, this book offers comprehensive information about participation in and attitudes toward academic governance. The authors examine the role of the academic department, summarize the effects of unionization, discuss what has become of the "community of scholars," and analyze what has happened to institutional diversity.

30 Carnegie Foundation for the Advancement of Teaching. *The Control of the Campus: A Report on the Governance of Higher Education.* Washington, D.C.: Carnegie Foundation for the Advancement of Teaching, 1982. 126 pages.

This essay takes a comprehensive look at the governance of American higher education, its roots, and how decision making is continuously affected by current conditions. It also examines the impact of regional and national associations, unions, and the government, as well as the role of trustees and the impact of the courts. It concludes that "the ever-increasing role of outside agencies in campus matters is gradually wearing down internal governance structures" and that "this destructive cycle must be ended." Future governance frameworks are also suggested.

★**31** Corson, John J. *The Governance of Colleges and Universities: Modernized Structures and Processes.* (Rev. ed.) New York: McGraw-Hill, 1975. 297 pages.

A comprehensive treatment of the organization, administration, and governance of colleges and universities, this book examines the whole of the institution, as well as the interrelationships between the parts, and how these are related to individual processes taking place within and between universities. Corson deals with how each major activity is governed and discusses how such compelling issues as unionization, state coordination, and financial difficulties affect institutional governance. This revised edition illuminates the changes that occurred from the 1960s to the mid 1970s.

★**32** Fisher, James L. *Power of the Presidency.* New York: Macmillan/American Council on Education, 1984. 206 pages.

Fisher, past president of CASE and a former college president, presents a review of the research on leadership and power, as well as his own insights. He explores the effectiveness of different types of power (charismatic, expert, legitimate, reward, and coercive) available to leaders within the context of typical situations faced by a college president. Of particular interest are the sections on public relations, fund raising, and alumni relations.

33 Kauffman, Joseph F. *At the Pleasure of the Board.* Riverside, N.J.: Macmillan, 1981. 122 pages.

This work examines the role of the college and university president, including myths, expectations, and realities of the presidency. Data are gathered from research studies, interviews with many presidents, and the author's personal experience as a college president. Among the issues discussed are presidential selection and evaluation, the relationship between the governing board and the president, problems of leadership in multicampus systems, collective bargaining, and the personal side of the presidency. The author examines several requirements for effective leadership in higher education, such as political effectiveness, aspects of visible leadership, the ability to teach the public, and a sense of service to the human spirit.

34 Nason, John W. *Presidential Assessment.* Washington, D.C.: Association of Governing Boards of Universities and Colleges, 1980. 86 pages.

This volume, a companion to Nason's *Presidential Search* (entry number 35), examines tested procedures used to assess presidential performance and demonstrates ways to establish sound guidelines. Nason presumes that periodic evaluation of presidential performance will both help the president and strengthen the institution.

35 Nason, John W. *Presidential Search.* Washington, D.C.: Association of Governing Boards of Universities and Colleges, 1982. 92 pages.

Since the first responsibility of any board of trustees is the selection and appointment of the president, this book will be a valuable asset to board members. Nason provides a practical nine-step guide through the selection process, from establishing the search machinery to making the final choice.

The Student

★**36**   Astin, Alexander W. *Four Critical Years: Effects of College on Beliefs, Attitudes, and Knowledge.* San Francisco: Jossey-Bass, 1977. 293 pages.

It is important for the advancement practitioner to be informed about all aspects of the students on the campus, both as an important internal constituency and as future alumni. Astin's work provides an analysis of how college affects students, based on a major ten-year study of more than 200,000 students and 300 institutions that represent all types of colleges and universities. The study records and analyzes findings from measures of more than eighty outcomes, covering student attitudes, self-concepts, values, aspirations, behavior patterns, persistence, achievement, competency, career development, and satisfaction. The research shows how outcomes are affected by contrasting college types and sheds light on the degree and intensity of college impacts, their durability, and their relation to career choices and future earnings.

37   Astin, Alexander W. *Achieving Educational Excellence: A Critical Assessment of Priorities and Practices in Higher Education.* San Francisco: Jossey-Bass, 1985. 254 pages.

This book shows how traditional views of excellence have led to counterproductive conformity in American colleges and universities. The author presents a new view of excellence as a development of student and faculty talent and details specific strategies for promoting student learning. Theories speak to increased student involvement and the methods that faculty and administrators can apply to improve the educational opportunities of their students. The book describes measures to promote good teaching and improve student service programs in response to changing aspirations and values.

38   Chickering, Arthur W. *Education and Identity*. San Francisco: Jossey-Bass, 1969. 367 pages.

This three-part volume describes the major dimensions of student development, the major aspects of college environments, and educational practices that influence them. Basic concepts and recommendations that might help strengthen the ways in which higher education facilitates developmental change are outlined and discussed.

39   Feldman, Kenneth A., and Newcomb, Theodore M. *The Impact of College on Students*. San Francisco: Jossey-Bass, 1969. Vol. 1, 474 pages. Vol. 2, 171 pages.

This two-volume set is a comprehensive presentation of 1,500 published and unpublished research reports on higher education and college students. Volume 1 contains a review and analysis of the findings, and volume 2 presents specific statistical information. This definitive compendium of research covers such issues as differences between college graduates and those who did not attend college, changes in student attitudes and values, the impact of faculty, type of curriculum, and residential and nonresidential experiences.

40   Kaplan, Martin (ed.). *What Is an Educated Person?: The Decades Ahead*. New York: Praeger, 1980. 195 pages.

This book, a thoughtful exploration of what the term "educated person" means in today's world and will mean in the future, is the product of two meetings, both organized by the Aspen Institute, in which a number of intellectuals from all sectors of world society discussed this question and includes papers and transcripts of actual discussions. Contributors include Mortimer J. Adler, Jerome Kegan, Adam Yarmolinsky, and William J. Bouwsma.

★**41**   Levine, Arthur. *When Dreams and Heroes Died: A Portrait of Today's College Student.* San Francisco: Jossey-Bass, 1980. 157 pages.

This report for the Carnegie Council on Policy Studies in Higher Education provides a description of today's undergraduates, based on surveys of 95,000 students, surveys of administrators at 870 colleges and universities, and campus visits to twenty-six institutions. It includes in-depth interviews with representative student groups and student leaders. The work compares popular stereotypes of college students in the 1960s and 1970s with realities about them, and highlights discrepancies between myth and fact. The study explores students' educational and social interests, political attitudes and behavior, the state of campus activism, and reports students' hopes and fears for their own future and that of the nation.

★**42**   Riesman, David. *On Higher Education: The Academic Enterprise in an Era of Rising Student Consumerism.* San Francisco: Jossey-Bass, 1981. 421 pages.

Through historical analysis, this report for the Carnegie Council on Policy Studies in Higher Education describes faculty dominance in the 1950s and early 1960s and the rise of student dissatisfaction in the latter 1960s and 1970s. It examines the consequences of growing student sovereignty as institutions compete for student customers, considers litigation against colleges by students and analyzes its impact on teaching and learning, and points to the danger of student consumerism and institutional acceptance of it. The book includes chapters on the role of accrediting associations in improving higher education and the role of students in shaping educational change.

Career Preparation and Development
of Advancement Professionals

★**43**   American College Public Relations Association. *The Advancement of Understanding and Support of Higher Education: A Conference of Organizational Principles and Patterns of College and University Relations Held at the Greenbrier.* Washington, D.C.: Council for Advancement and Support of Education, 1958. 83 pages.

This book is based on a study conducted by the American College Public Relations Association and the American Alumni Council, marking the beginning of institutional advancement as it is presently defined. The study identified the areas of public relations, alumni relations, and financial support programs as being of growing importance and, because of the interrelatedness of these functions, recommended that institutions provide for organizational and administrative coordination among them. Rather than describing a single "best" model, the book turns its attention to the development of specific institutional patterns and increased financial support of various related activities.

44   Council for Advancement and Support of Education. "Working with Consultants." *CASE Currents,* 1981, 7 (2), 22-32.

This special insert to *CASE Currents* offers general advice on how and when to use consultants. It describes location, selection, and agreement procedures and gives specific advice on using an outside designer or photographer.

45   Council for Advancement and Support of Education. "Institutional Advancement Survey." *CASE Currents,* 1982, *8* (6), 26-38.

This special twelve-page section of *CASE Currents* offers the first detailed examination of salaries and positions in institutional advancement. Based on a nationwide survey with 928 respondents, the report includes job responsibilities, reporting relationships, characteristics of member colleges and universities, and a breakdown of salaries by sex, age, and years of experience.

46 Council for Advancement and Support of Education. *Advancing Your Career.* Washington, D.C.: Council for Advancement and Support of Education, 1983. 11 pages.

This work examines job changes from the perspectives of an executive recruiter and a recent job hunter, provides tips on resumé writing, and offers advice from an advancement professional on building a career. It also includes a list of resources.

47 Reck, W. Emerson. *The Changing World of College Relations: History and Philosophy, 1917-1975.* Washington, D.C.: Council for Advancement and Support of Education, 1976. 473 pages.

This book describes the history, development, and organization of the American College Public Relations Association (ACPRA)—a national association of higher education professionals working in the areas of public relations, fund raising, alumni relations, and government relations.

48 Smith, Joel P. "Professionals in Development: Dignity or Disdain?" *CASE Currents,* 1984, *10* (8), 23-24.

In this article, a plea for professionalism and ethics in fund raising, Smith points to the need for standards and educational pathways for the profession. He cites the following characteristics as necessary for an advancement practitioner to claim professional respect: industry (hard work), resourcefulness (intelligence and common sense), resilience, personal perspective (humor), assertiveness, academic respect, institutional respect, knowledge, and integrity.

49   Stein, Ronald H., and Baca, M. Carlota (eds.). *Professional Ethics in University Administration.* New Directions for Higher Education, no. 33. San Francisco: Jossey-Bass, 1981. 272 pages.

This book examines some of the major ethical issues confronting academic administrators, including marketing abuse, sexual harassment, discrimination, and low academic standards. It discusses the responsibilities of administrators and academic institutions for self-regulation.

50   Willmer, Wesley K., and Rowland, A. Westley. "What Should You Read: The Literature of Institutional Advancement." *CASE Currents,* 1979, 5 (8), 30–32.

This article addresses the need for advancement professionals to know not only the literature of advancement but related publications in higher education as well. This is an important article for advancement practitioners who want to establish a good background in the various aspects of higher education.

General

★51   Helmken, Charles M. (ed.). *Best CASE Book.* Washington, D.C.: Council for Advancement and Support of Education, 1984. 183 pages.

This publication is a milestone in the fifty-six-year history of the Recognition Program, a multifaceted program sponsored by CASE and its predecessor organizations to recognize achievement by member institutions. It presents a summary of the ideas and information from the top advancement programs in the country as well as a photographic sampling of the finest periodicals and publications. Advancement practitioners interested in particular prize-winning programs may wish to contact the appropriate institutions for further information on how to adopt, adapt, or otherwise pursue their creative and successful ideas.

52 Muller, Steven. "Prologue: The Definition and Philosophy of Institutional Advancement." In A. Westley Rowland (gen. ed.), *Handbook of Institutional Advancement: A Practical Guide to College and University Relations, Fund Raising, Alumni Relations, Government Relations, Publications, and Executive Management for Continued Advancement.* (2nd ed.) San Francisco: Jossey-Bass, 1986. 12 pages.

In his prologue, Muller, president of Johns Hopkins University, sets the tone of the entire work with his definition and philosophy of institutional advancement. He discusses the nature of higher education in the United States and outlines the role of advancement in it, stressing that the function of advancement is to enable each individual college or university to succeed in a competitive environment and to assist the whole sector of higher education to compete effectively for available resources. An important part of this overview is his discussion of the relationship of the chief advancement officer to the president of the institution. (For a description of the *Handbook* in its entirety, see entry number 54.)

★53 Richards, Michael D., and Sherratt, Gerald R. *Institutional Advancement Strategies in Hard Times.* AAHE-ERIC Higher Education Research Report no. 2. Washington, D.C.: Clearinghouse on Higher Education, 1981. 49 pages.

This publication provides a description of the problems facing institutional advancement and examines four broad strategies: advancement as resource management, advancement programs built around institutional prestige, the use of marketing in institutional advancement, and the "flexible management" strategy, which combines features of the first three. The authors recommend this last approach.

★**54**   Rowland, A. Westley (gen. ed.). *Handbook of Institutional Advancement: A Practical Guide to College and University Relations, Fund Raising, Alumni Relations, Government Relations, Publications, and Executive Management for Continued Advancement.* (2nd ed.) San Francisco: Jossey-Bass, 1986. 656 pages. (1st ed., 1977, 577 pages.)

Sponsored by the Council for Advancement and Support of Education, this handbook was the first to deal comprehensively with the entire field of institutional advancement. It was compiled to provide advancement practitioners with essential information to aid in maintaining public confidence in colleges and universities and ensuring continued financial support, covering the areas of institutional relations, fund raising, alumni administration, government relations, publications, and executive management. The second edition of the *Handbook* is in reality a new book, more than 80 percent of which is new material. The updated information it contains about advancement reflects the maturing of the field and recent changes in professional philosophy and techniques within it. In addition to the topics covered in the first edition, this updated volume addresses new issues, including technology in advancement, enrollment management, speech writing, periodicals, the chief executive and advancement, advancement programs for two-year colleges, independent schools, and small and developing institutions, law and advancement, and market research. This is an indispensable resource for all advancement practitioners.

The Use of Volunteers

★**55**   Council for Advancement and Support of Education. "Volunteers." *CASE Currents*, 1978, *4* (entire issue 3).

This special issue of *CASE Currents* offers tips on how to recruit, train, manage, evaluate, and recognize volunteers for fund raising, alumni, public relations, and lobbying activities.

56 Gurin, Maurice G. *What Volunteers Should Know for Successful Fund Raising.* New York: Stein and Day, 1981. 151 pages.

This book, useful for volunteers and professionals alike, clarifies conventional fund-raising techniques and introduces new concepts and practices. It explores the relationship between volunteer and professional, emphasizing the need for reasonable expectations and mutual understanding of each other.

★57 Maddalena, Lucille A. (ed.). *Encouraging Voluntarism and Volunteers.* New Directions for Institutional Advancement, no. 9. San Francisco: Jossey-Bass, 1980. 95 pages.

This book presents criteria for determining when and how to employ alumni, trustees, and other volunteers in advancement activities. It outlines strategies and techniques for recruiting and managing volunteers so that they make effective and satisfying contributions. In his chapter on "Voluntarism: A New Age and a New Term of Volunteer Involvement in Higher Education," Arthur C. Frantzreb outlines eleven important questions confronting trustees, administrators, faculty, and staff; he points out the important role that the board of trustees plays in fund raising and emphasizes the function of the institutional advancement officer as a volunteer manager. Everyone who works with volunteers will want to read his seven rights of volunteers. Of special help to those who work with volunteers is the book's listing of additional reference sources.

58 Naylor, Harriet H. *Volunteers Today: Finding, Training, and Working with Them.* New York: Associates Press, 1967. 198 pages.

Written after twenty-five years of experience in volunteer programs, this book is full of Naylor's practical insights. It examines the principles of voluntarism and suggests ways to find, train, and manage volunteers in a variety of different settings and programs.

59 O'Connell, Brian (ed.). *America's Voluntary Spirit: A Book of Readings.* New York: Foundation Center, 1983. 450 pages.

This collection of forty-five readings celebrating and examining the richness and variety of the voluntary sector is a ready reference source containing some of the best speeches, articles, and papers on the subject. They dramatically illustrate the private philanthropy and voluntary actions that have contributed greatly to this country during the last 300 years.

60 Richards, Audrey. *Managing Volunteers for Results.* (2nd ed.) San Francisco: Public Management Institute, 1980. 350 pages.

This book uses a systems approach to teach techniques for creating a positive climate for volunteers. It discusses ways to recruit and motivate different kinds of volunteers and to become a more effective volunteer manager and describes a process for evaluating the effectiveness of a volunteer program. It includes hundreds of forms, checklists, and worksheets that assist in design and implementation.

★61 Smith, Virginia Carter, and Alberger, Patricia L. (eds.). *Involving Volunteers in Your Advancement Program.* Washington, D.C.: Council for Advancement and Support of Education, 1983. 112 pages.

This collection of *CASE Currents* articles on how to involve volunteers in an advancement program provides practical information on recruiting and managing volunteers and the use of trustees and board members as volunteers. It explores volunteer involvement in fund raising, public relations, student recruitment, government relations, and career assistance programs, with a section of volunteers' own statements on why they volunteer and what they need to continue and be successful.

62 Stenzel, Anne K., and Feeney, Helen M. *Volunteer Training and Development: A Manual.* (Rev. ed.) New York:
Seabury Press, 1976. 204 pages.

A practical manual designed for anyone involved in setting up
volunteer programs or in training volunteers, this book provides
advice on how to develop volunteer training programs and handle
the recruitment and replacement of volunteers. It discusses ways to
provide for continuation of volunteer learning and for the
development of educational leadership skills and includes information on evaluating individual learning and training programs.

63 Wilson, Marlene. *The Effective Management of Volunteer
Programs.* Boulder, Colo.: Volunteer, 1977. 197 pages.

This practical and useful guide to the management of volunteer
programs includes many helpful hints and good advice on
recruiting, training, and scheduling. It provides helpful lists,
charts, and sample forms that can be adapted to the needs of the
individual practitioner.

Trustees' Role in Advancement

64 Chait, Richard P., Taylor, Barbara, and Wood, Miriam.
Trustee Responsibility for Academic Affairs. Washington,
D.C.: Association of Governing Boards of Universities and
Colleges, 1985. 144 pages.

This book, tailored for college and university officials, covers the
areas of academic programs, personnel, budgets, and policies,
emphasizing the shaping of policy rather than administrative
detail. It discusses the role and responsibilities of the academic
affairs committee and offers guidelines for effective operations.
Appendixes include a self-study questionnaire, rational survey
results, and case studies.

★**65**   Council for Advancement and Support of Education. "Trustees in Fund Raising." *CASE Currents,* 1981, 7 (entire issue 4).

This special *CASE Currents* issue covers all aspects of trustee involvement in development, including identifying and cultivating prospective board members, relationships between development officers and trustees, and roles of trustees in fund raising and policy making.

★**66**   Frantzreb, Arthur C. (ed.). *Trustee's Role in Advancement.* New Directions for Institutional Advancement, no. 14. San Francisco: Jossey-Bass, 1981. 103 pages.

This book points out how the trustees of colleges and universities can be effectively used in institutional advancement activities. It discusses the function of trustees in planned gift programs and in such other fund-raising ventures as capital campaigns, operational support programs, and endowment programs.

★**67**   Gale, Robert L. *Building a More Effective Board.* Washington, D.C.: Association of Governing Boards of Universities and Colleges, 1984. 20 pages.

This is a short essay on how to build a strong board of trustees, which begins by selecting good people and educating them early and well.

★**68**   Heilbron, Louis H. *The College and University Trustee: A View from the Board Room.* San Francisco: Jossey-Bass, 1973. 239 pages.

Focusing on public boards of trustees, this book examines such issues as board composition and balance, appropriate areas for board policy, the board's role in dealing with sensitive issues, and board administration. It also discusses relationships with the president and college administrators, understanding of faculty and students, fund raising, public relations, and multi-institutional coordinating boards, or "superboards." The role of the trustee has become increasingly complex, and, along with detailed analyses of purposes, organization, and functions of boards, Heilbron presents recommendations for reform.

69 Herron, Orley R., Jr. *The Role of the Trustee.* Scranton, Pa.: International Textbook, 1969. 178 pages.

This book discusses the changing roles of trustees amid the shuffling of authority and power on the campus. It speaks to such issues of effective administration as shared decision making, political relationships, and the making of governing boards into more knowledgeable partners of the academic enterprise. Several case studies and recommendations, applicable to a wide range of educational institutions, are presented, along with techniques that are easily transferable to other institutions. It is designed as a textbook and tool for administrative personnel.

★70 Ingram, Richard T., and Associates. *Handbook of College and University Trusteeship: A Practical Guide for Trustees, Chief Executives, and Other Leaders Responsible for Developing Effective Governing Boards.* San Francisco: Jossey-Bass, 1980. 514 pages.

This book discusses all aspects of college and university trusteeship and provides a practical guide for chief executives and board members in fulfilling obligations to their institutions and the public. It synthesizes what is known about how governing boards function and how they should function, dispels myths and popular misconceptions about the roles of trustees, and clarifies trustee responsibilities, translating them into alternative policies and practices. It contains practical suggestions on how board members can maintain and improve working relationships with each other and with faculty, students, alumni, and other bodies.

71 Lord, James Gregory. *The Raising of Money: Thirty-Five Essentials Every Trustee Should Know.* Cleveland, Ohio: Third Sector Press, 1984. 128 pages.

This succinct and lucid book covers the theories and techniques of basic fund raising. It discusses key principles such as why and how people give, how campaigns can help people give, how to ask for gifts and follow them up, and how to utilize professional help. Written for board members, it also includes a coordinated guide for using the book with trustees.

72 Mueller, Robert Kirk. *Behind the Boardroom Door.* New York: Crown, 1984. 242 pages.

Recommended for college and university trustees and chief executives, this book makes the point that what happens behind the corporate boardroom door is precisely what happens behind any boardroom door—including the academy's. It compares the for-profit and not-for-profit sectors in terms of directors' freedom to act and challenges various models of organizational governance and their relevance to the changing American society, as well as the myth that higher education should more closely follow the corporate model. Combining elements from a number of disciplines, the author calls attention to performance reviews, meeting behaviors, stakeholders, shareholders, ethics, and the maintenance of independence and objectivity.

73 Nason, John W. *The Future of Trusteeship: The Role and Responsibilities of College and University Boards.* A report of the Commission on the Future of the Association of Governing Boards of Universities and Colleges. Washington, D.C.: Association of Governing Boards of Universities and Colleges, 1974. 40 pages.

An examination of the role and responsibilities of trustees and regents of institutions of higher education in the United States during the last quarter of the twentieth century, this report lists ten major responsibilities trustees face in the future, including clarification of purpose, enhancement of public relations, assessment of performance, and preservation of institutional independence. Based on the results of a study on what circumstances or combinations of circumstances make some boards successful and others not, the report also lists eleven factors that can increase the strength and effectiveness of board performance if the boards are prepared to rise to the responsibilities.

★**74** Nason, John W. *The Nature of Trusteeship.* Washington, D.C.: Association of Governing Boards of Universities and Colleges, 1982. 136 pages.

This classic text is an insightful examination of the widening roles trustees are called upon to fulfill and the challenges they must overcome. The author explains the thirteen major responsibilities of governing boards and explores fourteen organizational factors that control effectiveness.

75 Nason, John W. *Trustee Responsibilities.* Washington, D.C.: Association of Governing Boards of Universities and Colleges, 1985. 16 pages.

This is a valuable guide to the thirteen basic responsibilities of governing board members.

76 National Commission on College and University Trustee Selection. *Recommendations for Improving Trustee Selection in Public Colleges and Universities.* Washington, D.C.: Association of Governing Boards of Universities and Colleges, 1980. 54 pages.

This book is similar to the one described in entry number 74, with modifications made to suit the needs of public institutions.

77 Rauh, Morton A. *The Trusteeship of Colleges and Universities.* New York: McGraw-Hill, 1969. 206 pages.

Written for trustees, this book covers such topics as characteristics and responsibilities of trustees; relationships between the board and the president, faculty, students, and the public; finance and management; mechanics of board organization; and trusteeships in specific types of institutions—public, junior, and religious. Appendix A presents specific topics that have direct application to the management of most colleges, appendix B reports the results of a trustee survey taken in 1967.

78 Zwingle, J. L. *Effective Trusteeship.* (Rev. ed.) Washington, D.C.: Association of Governing Boards of Universities and Colleges, 1980. 42 pages.

In this book, Association of Governing Boards president emeritus J. L. Zwingle reports on ways to improve the performance of governing boards. He outlines the board's role, organization, and structure and discusses useful relationships among administrators, faculty, students, and the public. The book includes a bibliography on trusteeship as well as a self-explanatory trustee audit to help board members evaluate themselves.

Research and Evaluation

79 Babbie, E. R. *The Practice of Social Research.* (2nd ed.) Belmont, Calif.: Wadsworth, 1979. 596 pages.

This text on general research methods reviews the logic of social scientific inquiry, techniques of sampling, the variety of research designs available to social researchers, measurement and statistics, and consideration of research ethics. Each chapter contains examples from actual research projects.

★80 Barzun, Jacques, and Graf, Henry F. *Modern Researcher.* New York: Harcourt Brace Jovanovich, 1970. 430 pages.

This is a classic, highly readable discussion of the human aspects of research, especially in qualitative rather than quantitative forms. This book will inspire readers to enjoy a high degree of rigor in research work. It is aimed at anyone who is or will be engaged in research and report writing. The book concentrates on principles of thought and analysis of difficulties and illustrates both theory and practice by examples from many fields. The chapters on research include discussions of the searcher's mind and virtues; finding the facts; verification; handling ideas; truth and causation; pattern, bias; and great systems.

★**81**   Blalock, Hubert M., and Blalock, Ann (eds.). *Methodology in Social Research*. New York: McGraw-Hill, 1968. 493 pages.

This book offers a sophisticated treatment of methodological issues and problems characteristic of research in higher education. For those seeking a detailed, higher-level understanding of the methods of survey research, this book provides several excellent articles. Chapter 1 is a must for all.

82   Blankenship, Albert B. *Professional Telephone Surveys*. New York: McGraw-Hill, 1977. 244 pages.

Aimed at the generalist in marketing research, this book focuses on techniques of telephone surveying, including chapters on sampling, questionnaire construction and testing, interviewers and interviewing, data processing, and reporting. Introductory chapters describe how telephone surveys have come of age and describe the development of telephone surveys as a tool in survey research. Chapter 10 provides an interesting description of the future of professional telephone surveys, including continuing pressures to increase telephone surveys, the decline of mail and personal-interview surveys, and special concerns for the future, such as misleading uses of the telephone-survey approach, invasion of privacy, and mistreatment of the respondent.

83   Breen, George Edward. *Do-It-Yourself Marketing Research*. New York: McGraw-Hill, 1977. 258 pages.

Though intended for a business audience, this book has some useful information for education marketers, such as how to use mail questionnaires, boost percentage of returns, handle individual and group interviews, and make sure that samplings are accurate and valid. The final chapter, "Company 'Politics': How to Get Your Research Taken Seriously," is helpful to those who feel that their presidents do not listen to their advice.

★**84**   Carter, Virginia L. (ed.). *How to Survey Your Readers.*
Washington, D.C.: Council for Advancement and Support
of Education, 1981. 48 pages.

This publication contains information on what a readership
survey can do for a periodical, material on how to conduct a mail
survey, and nine sample questionnaires from institutions of
various sizes and types.

85   Cochran, William C. *Sampling Techniques.* (3rd ed.) New
York: Wiley, 1977. 428 pages.

This revision of a classic sampling text emphasizes theory and
mathematical rigor. Among the proofs and derivations, however,
are clear and concise prose explanations and descriptions that
should be very useful to people who are trying to design their own
first studies.

86   Council for Advancement and Support of Education.
Evaluating Your PR Program. Washington, D.C.: Council
for Advancement and Support of Education, 1984. 10
pages.

This publication points out the need for program evaluation in
measuring the effectiveness of public relations campaigns. It
explains how to practice public relations through use of objectives
and to evaluate news and other services accordingly.

87   Dexter, Lewis A. *Elite and Specialized Interviewing.*
Evanston, Ill.: Northwestern University Press, 1970. 205
pages.

This book was written specifically to provide guidelines to those
interviewing elite populations, such as corporation officials,
legislators, or high-level bureaucrats, which requires a different
approach from that used with general populations. The book
points out that elite interviews tend to be unstructured, with the
respondent given deference in the definition and structure of the
research situation.

★**88**   Dillman, Donald A. *Mail and Telephone Surveys: The Total Design Method.* New York: Wiley, 1978. 325 pages.

This is a comprehensive work on the design and implementation of mail and telephone surveys. The "total design method" (TDM) is an organizational plan that enumerates all tasks, from question design to personnel recruitment, necessary for successful completion. The book compares mail, telephone, and face-to-face surveys on several dimensions.

89   Douglas, Jack D. *Investigative Social Research: Individual and Team Field Research.* Beverly Hills, Calif.: Sage, 1976. 229 pages.

Rather than a discussion of surveys or statistics, this book offers another set of research methods available to get at truth in field research. Douglas discusses techniques of observation, interviewing, and conceptualization that are most appropriate when the researcher has decided to get closer to his or her population of interest by interacting with them in their natural social settings.

★**90**   Erdos, Paul L. *Professional Mail Surveys.* (Rev. ed.) New York: McGraw-Hill, 1984. 296 pages.

Techniques used for professional mail surveys are described in sufficient detail to enable readers to conduct their own surveys, to evaluate those made by others, or simply to become acquainted with proven procedures used in mail surveys. Topics of value to the advancement professional include types of mail surveys, survey design, mailing lists, questionnaire construction, cost estimating and scheduling, pilot studies, and advance notice of questionnaires. The chapter on evaluating mail surveys, which includes a fifty-six-point checklist, is particularly helpful. The book also discusses several areas that are still debated by professionals, including incentives, the accompanying letter, mailing procedures, and follow-up mailings.

★**91**   Francis, J. Bruce (ed.). *Surveying Institutional Constituen-*
         cies. New Directions for Institutional Advancement, no. 6.
         San Francisco: Jossey-Bass, 1979. 100 pages.

This sourcebook examines the survey as a method of gathering
accurate and reliable information about constituent views and
attitudes and explains how to organize that information so that it
is most useful to policy and decision makers. Discussion concerns
when the survey should be chosen as an appropriate strategy, the
available methods and techniques and their relative strengths and
weaknesses, and what steps might facilitate the successful carrying
out of survey methods. The section by Cletis Pride, "Building
Response to a Mail Survey," is excellent and should be read by
everyone. Other topics include the advantages and disadvantages of
different survey techniques, sampling, questionnaire design, and
data analysis. This is a must book for advancement professionals.

★**92**   Groves, Robert M., and Kahn, Robert L. *Surveys by*
         Telephone. New York: Academic Press, 1979. 358 pages.

This book describes an experimental evaluation of a major
development in the history of survey methods: sampling and
interviews by telephone. Telephone surveys are attractive: sampling random telephone numbers is relatively easy and inexpen-
sive, and conducting interviews by telephone is quick and
economical; telephone lines go where interviewers may fear to
tread and reach behind doors that householders may fear to open.
The opposing disadvantages are the long-recognized biases of
limited telephone coverage of household populations, the less-
known constraints of using the telephone system as a sampling
frame, and the largely unknown effects of the telephone medium
itself on the quality of interview data. The objective of this book is
to answer the questions that confront every researcher planning to
collect data from household populations—questions of error and
precision, costs and benefits, administration, and organization.
One very helpful section is the comparison of two major methods
of survey research, telephone and personal interviews, with respect
to a whole array of attributes—administrative arrangements, costs,
and components of error.

93 Halstead, Carol P. "Assessing the Performance of the Public Relations Office." In Robert A. Scott (ed.), *Determining the Effectiveness of Campus Services*. New Directions for Institutional Research, no. 41. San Francisco: Jossey-Bass, 1984. 13 pages.

The author points out that setting objectives and knowing how to evaluate results are particularly important factors in public relations, where it is easy to get caught up in counting news releases rather than assessing whether the target audience has been reached. Stating that the real test of a public relations program is its results, the author suggests asking: Did it pay off at the box office? in alumni clubs? in the development office? in the offices of foundation and corporate sponsors? in the accreditation review? in efforts to recruit high-quality faculty? in attracting grants for new programs, new services, new buildings, the endowment, financial aid? This work suggests criteria for evaluation and discusses several checkpoints in the evaluation process, with such questions as: Is the program adequately planned? Are the goals and objectives clearly stated? Have messages, slogans, and themes been carefully developed for each key audience? Has a strategy been developed for reaching goals and objectives? Have appropriate channels of communication been selected to reach key audiences in an efficient and effective manner? Does the program provide for monitoring and evaluation?

94 Henerson, Marlene E., Morris, Lynn Lyons, and Fitz-Gibbons, Carol Taylor. *How to Measure Attitudes*. Beverly Hills, Calif.: Sage, 1978. 184 pages.

While this book is part of a larger series on educational program evaluation, it contains specific information on the design, testing, and administration of surveys, much of which is relevant and useful to advancement officers.

★**95**   Jacobson, Harvey K. (ed.). *Evaluating Advancement Programs.* New Directions for Institutional Advancement, no. 1. San Francisco: Jossey-Bass, 1978. 117 pages.

This book analyzes procedures for evaluating institutional advancement, making clear what evaluation can accomplish, what the problems are, and how pitfalls can be detected and avoided. It presents guidelines and illustrative examples to help institutional advancement officers design their own evaluation studies, frame appropriate assignments for evaluation consultants, and use the information gathered to improve program decision making.

96   Johnston, Jerome (ed.). *Evaluating the New Information Technologies.* New Directions for Program Evaluation, no. 23. San Francisco: Jossey-Bass, 1984. 93 pages.

This book responds to the growing need for managers, educators, and individual consumers to effectively evaluate the proliferation of current information and communication technologies. It examines and compares a range of methods for evaluating microcomputers, electronic mail, videodisc, videotext, and teletext in terms of costs, quality.

★**97**   Kerlinger, Fred N. *Foundations of Behavioral Research.* (2nd ed.) New York: Holt, Rinehart & Winston, 1973. 739 pages.

This is a detailed but not overly sophisticated treatment of the major statistical and research design topics that researchers are likely to confront—a highly readable discussion of the logic of experimental design and analysis of variance. This is a book that should be read from cover to cover, then referred to again and again during actual research work.

98 Krech, David, and Crutchfield, Richard S. *Theory and Problems of Social Psychology.* New York: McGraw-Hill, 1948. 639 pages.

A text first published more than thirty-six years ago, this book contains two excellent chapters on opinion research. Chapter 7, "The Measurement of Beliefs and Attitudes," discusses theory of belief and attitude measurement; measurement by scales, including the Thurstone method of scale construction, the Likert method, the Guttman method, the Bogardus social-distance scale, and the rank-order scale; and measurement by ratings, as well as the reliability and validity of measurement of beliefs and attitudes. Chapter 8, "Public Opinion Research," includes such areas as development of large-scale methods of measurement, types of questions (the poll question, the open-ended question), problems of interviewing, sampling, problems of analysis, and steps in public opinion survey.

★**99** Lawler, Edward E. III, Mohrman, Allen M., Jr., Mohrman, Susan A., Ledford, Gerald E., Jr., Cummings, Thomas G., and Associates. *Doing Research That Is Useful for Theory and Practice.* San Francisco: Jossey-Bass, 1985. 400 pages.

This study gives recognized authorities in the organizational field the opportunity to present their approaches to performing research that is useful both for improving practice and for building scientific knowledge and theory. The seventeen experts also offer insightful commentary on the diverse research approaches of other authorities. This is a revealing analysis of how leaders in the field view the aims and methods of their own and others' research.

★**100** Lindenmann, Walter K. *Attitude and Opinion Research.* (2nd ed.) Washington, D.C.: Council for Advancement and Support of Education, 1981. 83 pages.

This publication outlines types of studies and professional services available for educators who are considering doing opinion research. The first chapter will be helpful to the advancement officer, as it covers basic forms of surveys, selecting an opinion-research organization, services offered by research organizations, shirttail studies, custom-tailored studies, and a checklist for academic communicators. The appendix includes tips for doing mail surveys and offers sample survey forms for such areas as alumni, community marketing, institutional image, student opinion, readership, student recruitment publications, and student recruitment marketing.

★**101** McKenna, Barbara (ed.). *Surveying Your Alumni: Guidelines and 22 Sample Questionnaires.* Washington, D.C.: Council for Advancement and Support of Education, 1983. 184 pages.

Keeping on top of where alumni live, what they are doing, and how they feel about the institution is an awesome task. In four sections, this handbook covers the entire process of conducting direct-mail or telephone surveys, including designing the survey, selecting a random sample, compiling data, and evaluating and reporting the results. It presents helpful survey techniques and samples of biographical and opinion-type questionnaires.

102 Parten, Mildred B. *Surveys, Polls, and Samples: Practical Procedures.* New York: Harper & Row, 1950. 624 pages.

This book is based on more than twenty years of active participation in social surveys and polling projects, and, although published more than thirty years ago, it is still highly regarded in the field. The surveys given primary consideration here are those conducted by questionnaires and similar techniques for gathering information about people rather than about community agencies or facilities provided for them. Emphasis is placed on specific procedures that provide the practical answers to the numerous technical problems arising at every stage of the survey operation. Thus, this is an overall guide for planning the survey, drafting the forms, writing the instructions, securing the information, and interpreting and reporting the results. Among the important topics covered are planning the procedure, methods of securing information, the role of sampling, construction of the schedule or questionnaire, types of sampling, size of sample, interview procedures, mail questionnaire procedures, sources of bias, tabulation of the data, and evaluation of the data and sample.

★**103** Pirsig, Robert M. *Zen and the Art of Motorcycle Maintenance*. Toronto: Bantam Books, 1974. 373 pages.

This is perhaps the most exciting and profoundly interesting treatment of the logic underlying research and rationality that exists in the English language. Using a novel format to provide a platform for presenting analyses of the major issues in philosophy of science, the author provides stunning insights into how researchers should approach their art and what pitfalls to avoid.

104 Public Management Institute. *Evaluation Handbook*. San Francisco: Public Management Institute, 1980. 400 pages.

This work explains how to design and conduct evaluations, covering such topics as how to use evaluation design to increase the "fundability" of proposals, data collection methods, and evaluation report design. It includes over 400 pages of forms, worksheets, and checklists, as well as sample evaluation designs, surveys, and reports that can be used as models.

105 Redding, W. Charles. *How to Conduct a Readership Survey*. Chicago: Lawrence Ragan Communications, 1982. 152 pages.

This publication offers guidelines to help determine whether a survey is needed and to make a survey accurate. It contains step-by-step instructions together with examples of the do's and don't's of survey methods. The major premise of this book is that bad information is worse than no information, and it offers practical and specific advice on how to get good information.

106 Rosenberg, Morris. *The Logic of Survey Analysis*. New York: Basic Books, 1968. 283 pages.

This work presents a detailed analysis of the logic of using data from surveys to draw conclusions about events and to develop theoretical explanations of them. Virtually no knowledge of statistics is assumed or required by this book, which nevertheless prepares one to understand and evaluate survey reports. This book is valuable both for researchers who will be analyzing data and for professionals who will be called upon to interpret the results and conclusions of researchers. It offers probably the best available treatment of table and graph interpretation.

★**107** Rowland, A. Westley. *Research in Institutional Advancement.* Washington, D.C.: Council for Advancement and Support of Education, 1983. 136 pages.

This work contains summaries of abstracts of 267 doctoral dissertations in institutional advancement, divided into six sections: institutional relations, educational fund raising, alumni administration, government relations, publications, and executive management. It also includes a sampling of master's theses on advancement topics. This is a relatively untapped source of information for advancement officers. Many of these dissertations offer results that advancement professionals can apply to their own problems and programs.

108 Schmidt, Marty. *Understanding and Using Statistics.* Lexington, Mass.: Heath, 1975. 361 pages.

This is a highly readable and direct explanation of statistical methods in everyday, nonmathematical language, with a particularly helpful explanation of chi-square statistics.

109 Sellitz, Claire, Wrightsman, Lawrence S., and Cooke, Stuart, W. *Research Methods in Social Relations.* New York: Holt, Rinehart & Winston, 1976. 624 pages.

This is a comprehensive collection of chapters treating every phase of research design for survey studies. It contains as an appendix the classic description by Kornhauser and Sheatsley of questionnaire construction and interview procedure.

110 Siegel, Sidney. *Non-Parametric Statistics.* New York: Basic
Books, 1956. 312 pages.

Although not very recent, this is still the most lucid and useful
reference on when and how to use statistics, designed for situations
that do not fit usual statistical assumptions (in some sense, this
includes all real-life situations). The book not only contains
descriptions of the methods and when they are appropriate, but
also provides step-by-step instructions for calculating and interpreting them.

111 Sudman, Seymour. *Applied Sampling.* New York: Academic Press, 1976. 249 pages.

Intended for researchers who have limited resources and statistical
backgrounds and who wish to maximize the usefulness of the data
they obtain, this book provides many examples of sampling
problems, from simple random sampling through complex
designs. It is generally very readable and considerably less
mathematical than most sampling books.

Marketing

112 Barton, David W., Jr. (ed.). *Marketing Higher Education.*
New Directions for Higher Education, no. 21. San Francisco: Jossey-Bass, 1978. 88 pages.

This book describes the interrelationship between the academic
program and the admissions operation. Five experienced admissions officers discuss four angles of marketing in terms of
communicating with prospective students.

★113 Council for Advancement and Support of Education.
"Market Research." *CASE Currents,* 1978, *4* (entire issue
5).

This special issue of *CASE Currents* covers types of research, such
as surveying alumni by mail or telephone, and how research
results can improve corporate relations programs, predict which

alumni will give, indicate which graphic treatments readers prefer, and help recruit more students.

114 Harper, Nancy. "Why We Need Marketing." *CASE Currents*, 1984, *10* (8), 30–33.

This article is the result of an interview with Harold T. Martin, professor of marketing in Northwestern University's Graduate School of Management. Martin responds to some nineteen questions about marketing for colleges and universities. He sees several benefits to be obtained from a marketing plan: better balancing of conflicting interests, a better monitoring of important changes in the environment, a more relevant product, and greater communication effectiveness.

115 Kotler, Philip, Ferrell, O. C., and Lamb, Charles. *Cases and Readings for Marketing for Nonprofit Organizations.* Englewood Cliffs, N.J.: Prentice-Hall, 1983. 380 pages.

This comprehensive series of articles and cases describes specific applications of marketing to nonprofit institutions and discusses the adaptation of marketing concept and theory. Two of the cases reported are taken from the academic world: Simon's Rock College and Kent State University.

★**116** Kotler, Philip, and Fox, Karen. *Strategic Marketing for Educational Institutions.* Englewood Cliffs, N.J.: Prentice-Hall, 1985. 416 pages.

This book presents various marketing concepts and tools that can be used to determine an institution's current situation and to make more informed judgments about programs and markets. It provides to-the-point advice on such crucial tasks as attracting students, increasing student satisfaction, and enlisting the support of alumni and contains a number of useful guidelines, vignettes, and diagrams based on the experiences of various schools, colleges, and universities. Sections cover the fundamentals of marketing, from planning the marketing process to evaluating marketing performance.

117 Lucas, John A. (ed.). *Developing a Total Marketing Plan.* New Directions for Institutional Research, no. 21. San Francisco: Jossey-Bass, 1979. 97 pages.

This sourcebook describes and illustrates how the total marketing concept can be applied to institutions of higher education. The total marketing concept involves a comprehensive plan utilizing two-way communication and the identification of specific target groups for specific programs.

118 Montana, Patrick J. (ed.). *Marketing in Nonprofit Organizations.* New York: American Management Association, 1978. 392 pages.

This work is a collection of articles from journals and magazines published between 1972 and 1978. Several of these deal directly with college and university marketing concepts, and nearly all of them are useful to college and university administrators. The book suggests that the basic problem of education is overcapacity and that success depends on having a "competitive advantage." Among the marketing research efforts discussed are studies of student attitudes, exit interviews, institutional image, and "educational program focus groups."

119 Nash, Edward L. (ed.). *The Direct Marketing Handbook.* New York: McGraw-Hill, 1984. 928 pages.

This collection of sixty top direct-marketing experts' insights contains hundreds of professional tips applicable to nonprofit and profit-making groups and an extensive selection of new ideas for fund raisers, featuring articles on strategic planning, market research, creative promotion, effective letter writing, production costs, and budgeting.

120 Pride, Cletis, and Fowler, Joseph S. "Chapter 59: Market Research: The Starting Point for Advancement Success." In A. Westley Rowland (gen. ed.), *Handbook of Institutional Advancement: A Practical Guide to College and University Relations, Fund Raising, Alumni Relations, Government Relations, Publications, and Executive Management for Continued Advancement.* (2nd ed.) San Francisco: Jossey-Bass, 1986. 21 pages.

After defining what market research is, the authors discuss such topics as doing it yourself, exploring secondary sources, the roles of qualitative and quantitative research, sampling, questionnaire design, mail, telephone, and interview surveys, and managing the project. (For a description of the *Handbook* in its entirety, see entry number 54.)

121 Rados, David L. *Marketing for Non-Profit Organizations.* Boston: Auburn House, 1981. 572 pages.

This textbook can assist those in nonprofit organizations to better analyze marketing problems and to devise solutions that recognize the financial costs and benefits of different marketing approaches. Chapters are devoted to such topics as marketing costs, marketing controls and organization, marketing strategy, market research, and communications. The book discusses the application of marketing to fund raising and uses examples from higher education as well as other nonprofit organizations.

122 Smith, Virginia Carter, and Garigan, Catherine S. (eds.). *A Marketing Approach to Student Recruitment.* Washington, D.C.: Council for Advancement and Support of Education, 1979. 79 pages.

This collection of forty-six *CASE Currents* articles on the use of marketing in student recruitment covers such topics as what marketing is, how to conduct market research, student consumerism, advertising, publications, and the use of alumni, students, and the media in student recruitment.

123 Stone, Bob. *Successful Direct Marketing Methods.* (2nd ed.) Chicago: Crain Books, 1979. 370 pages.

A practical work on direct-marketing methods, this book covers examples and case histories of actual companies and includes approximately a hundred illustrations of effective ads. Chapter topics include starting a direct-marketing operation, choosing the right media for the marketing message, and creating and producing direct-marketing materials, direct-mail packages, catalogues, and print advertisements. This edition also contains new material on mailing lists, broadcast techniques, telephone marketing, and current techniques for catalogue preparation and distribution.

★**124** Topor, Robert S. *Marketing in Higher Education: A Practical Guide.* Washington, D.C.: Council for Advancement and Support of Education, 1983. 103 pages.

This publication offers a guide to applying marketing concepts and techniques to the needs of various educational constituencies (students, donors, supporters, alumni) in order to improve products, services, and communications. It identifies ways to tailor activities to customer needs and explains how to build strong communications that promote activities. Specific chapters deal with market research, audience segmentation, image, positioning your institution, marketing strategy, defining your institution, communications, and making marketing work.

★**125** Topor, Robert S. *Institutional Image: How to Define, Improve, Market It.* Washington, D.C.: Council for Advancement and Support of Education, 1986. 68 pages.

This publication provides an in-depth look at institutional image. No matter how impressions are formed, the author contends that people's perceptions are critical to institutional well-being. Because of an increasingly competitive future for education institutions, he stresses that image will become even more significant. This work discusses many important matters of concern to advancement officers as they communicate the image of their institution. Starting with two key questions—What determines image? and What is quality?—the author discusses identifying an institution's image, creating an image program, and marketing an institutional image.

The Use of Computers in Advancement

126 Council for Advancement and Support of Education. "Computers." *CASE Currents,* 1978, *4* (entire issue 8).

This special issue of *CASE Currents* focuses on the use of computers in institutional advancement. It includes general advice as well as specific applications to fund raising, alumni relations, public relations, government relations, publications, and institutional management. It also includes a helpful glossary.

127 Council for Advancement and Support of Education. "Computers in Alumni and Development." *CASE Currents,* 1983, *9* (entire issue 3).

Another special issue of *CASE Currents* devoted to the usefulness of computers in alumni relations and development, this publication provides detailed information on applications such as computer models that make annual giving predictions, using available technology to increase results from direct-mail fund raising, and how to link a word processor and computer. It includes articles on the use of computers in independent schools, how to plan and implement computer conversions, and how to instruct users in developing an efficient computer system.

128 Gilman, Kenneth. *Computer Resource Guide for Nonprofits.* (2nd ed.) San Francisco: Public Management Institute, 1984. 700 pages.

The first part of this book is a directory of software, designed to help nonprofit agencies decide which software matches their particular needs. It contains reports on 205 software programs in the major categories of fund-raising software, financial software, and constituent services and lists software for twenty-five different micros, eleven different minis, and four major mainframes. The second part is a directory of foundations, corporations, and federal agencies that offer grants for computer hardware, software, and training.

3

Institutional Relations

Institutional relations is the interpretative arm of advancement—the area that focuses on public relations and the overall communications program of a college or university as it seeks to gain understanding and support from its varied constituencies. Every college or university has at least twenty or thirty constituencies, internal and external. The public relations program of an institution consists of a variety of activities and communications to secure the understanding and support of these publics. In addition, the advancement professional serves as a consultant to administrators, faculty and staff, and students about potential public relations results of policy decisions. An effective public relations program will assist in analyzing, interpreting, and, most importantly, anticipating public opinion, attitudes, and issues that might affect the operation of the institution.

As with charity, an effective program of institutional relations for a college or university must begin at home—that is, on the campus. It is generally agreed by experienced practitioners in the field that what happens on the campus and what those who study and work there say and think about the institution may well be more important than any external efforts. Thus, the students, faculty, and staff are key publics in the communication process of interpreting an institution. The morale of the faculty, the feeling of "oneness" with the institution, the students' attitude toward the faculty and administration, and the general esprit de corps on the campus are based on a multitude of factors, all important and all combining to produce effective internal relations. A college or university can set a positive tone for its internal relations through clearly stated institutional objectives, such as a commitment to academic freedom and participation in community activities. A calendar of campus events, a fact book about the institution, campus motion pictures or slides, a president's open-door policy for students, faculty and staff, a suggestion system, campus bulletin boards, and provision of adequate parking can all contribute to a positive climate on the campus.

As new members are appointed to faculty and staff, they can be sent special materials (such as letters of welcome, a campus map, a faculty-staff handbook, and an explanation of benefits), and they and their families can be introduced to the institution at a special orientation meeting. Positive relations with faculty and staff can be maintained by providing a competitive salary schedule and a good program of benefits (a comprehensive hospital and surgical plan; employer-financed retirement and life insurance programs; reduced tuition for children of faculty and professional staff; a credit union), maintaining ongoing communication through a calendar of campus events, faculty-staff meetings where institutional plans and policies are presented, an annual financial report, closed-circuit campus radio and television, and an annual "state of the university" address by the president, and recognizing the importance of teaching and research to the institution by providing adequate office space and support staff (including graduate assistants and fellows as well as stenographic and clerical staff) and adequate facilities and support for research.

A recreational program for faculty and staff and their families, financial assistance to encourage attendance at conferences, recognition of retirees, a faculty-staff magazine, an emeritus club, a faculty club, assignment to faculty committees, and an annual faculty-staff reception, picnic, or dinner are all additional ways to maintain positive relations with this internal public.

The institution can foster a positive attitude among its students by providing a broad program of student services (placement, activities, health, and counseling), encouraging student participation in policy decisions, including students in institutional committees, and making important institutional publications available to them. A viable student government, a student roundtable or forum for airing complaints, a student newspaper, and fair and equitable regulations are also effective in contributing to positive relations with students.

An institution's external relations program is concerned with individuals and groups beyond the campus—alumni, parents of students, the governing board, legislators, the news media, donors, merchants, service industries, minority groups, labor unions, business executives and chambers of commerce, local government and public and private school officials, religious groups, other colleges and universities, health care providers, women's groups, social organizations, and the general public. Programs for these groups must be tailor-made to respond to their individual needs. Typical of programs for this purpose are press conferences and news releases; television and radio programs; annual motion pictures; special publications and programs for alumni; a president's newsletter; a parents' association and newsletter; special events; displays and exhibits; campus tours and open houses; a speakers' bureau; a community advisory council; and university-community dialogues.

Institutional communication is considered by many to be the most important process in any organization. Organizations that effectively create and exchange messages, both within their systems and between themselves and their environments, will survive and thrive; those that do not will ultimately die. This principle is illustrated especially at institutions of higher education, where the rapidly changing environment has created new information demands on the colleges and universities of the nation. An effective program of advancement depends heavily on effective communication, both written and spoken. The ability of the advancement officer to communicate effectively, in both speaking and writing, will largely determine his or her success. Effective communication is the heart of management, fund raising, institutional relations, government relations, publications, and enrollment management. First and foremost, advancement practitioners must be effective communicators.

Advancement professionals who work in institutional relations are concerned with internal and external communications programs, the print and electronic media, special events, campus and community relations, speech writing, and the effective use of photography. In addition to a selection of works of general interest in institutional relations, this chapter presents a variety of publications covering these special areas, dealing with both theory and practice and giving special consideration to the barriers that disrupt effective communication.

General

★**129** Alberger, Patricia L., and Carter, Virginia L. (eds.). *Communicating University Research.* Washington, D.C.: Council for Advancement and Support of Education, 1981. 226 pages.

This book covers the handling of controversial research, the public's perception of research, reaching specific audiences, working with the media, and related topics. Journalists from newspapers, wire services, magazines, radio, and television describe how they cover topics in science. The work also contains articles based on presentations at CASE's 1980 conference on this subject and includes a suggested reading list.

130 Aronoff, Craig E., and Bashin, Otis W. *Public Relations: The Profession and the Practice.* St. Paul, Minn.: West, 1983. 466 pages.

This book deals with public relations in the overall context of organizational communications. It stresses the practitioner's role in organizational and societal communication systems and examines the challenges to the profession both from within organizations and from surrounding environments. The six sections cover such topics as the profession, the process of public relations, the publics of public relations, and public relations in nonprofit as well as business organizations. Critical issues such as social responsibility, consumerism, and environmentalism are also discussed.

131 Balthaser, William. *Successful Public Relations Techniques.* San Francisco: Public Management Institute, 1982. 450 pages.

This manual contains a wealth of information on public relations techniques to increase an organization's visibility and improve relations with external constituencies. The manual shows how to create newsworthy events and deal effectively with the media; how to issue news releases, public service announcements, and informative brochures; and how to coordinate public relations with fund raising.

132 Bernays, Edward L. *Engineering of Consent.* Norman: University of Oklahoma Press, 1969. 246 pages.

Eight experts in the field of public relations discuss the central problem of gaining popular acceptance for ideas, programs, or innovative courses of action. This is a systematic illustration of the principal organizational problems facing any public relations undertaking.

★**133** Butterfield, William H. *How to Use Letters in College Public Relations: A Survey of Principles and Source Book of Effective Examples.* New York: Harper & Row, 1944. 112 pages.

This book points out some of the best opportunities to utilize personal letters and illustrates effective procedures for realizing the maximum results from them. It discusses the types with the greatest potential for being effective and provides examples of letters written by college and university professionals to alumni and business and professional representatives. Letters designed to elicit support for junior colleges are discussed in the appendix.

134 Center, Allen H., and Walsh, Frank E. *Public Relations Practices: Managerial Case Studies and Problems.* (3rd ed.) Englewood Cliffs, N.J.: Prentice-Hall, 1984. 350 pages.

This book contains forty-two open-ended case studies and discussions of thirty-seven on-the-job problems arranged in

workbook fashion, geared to increasing public relations skills. It
also includes a chapter on career preparation, full of handy tips.

135 Ciervo, Arthur V. (ed.). "Part One: Institutional Relations." In A. Westley Rowland (gen. ed.), *Handbook of
Institutional Advancement: A Practical Guide to College
and University Relations, Fund Raising, Alumni Relations, Publications, and Executive Management for
Continued Advancement.* (1st ed.) San Francisco: Jossey-
Bass, 1977. 109 pages.

This part of the *Handbook,* concerned with the public relations of
colleges and universities, presents an excellent analysis of the
characteristics of a professional in college and university public
relations and discusses short-term and long-term public relations
goals of typical institutions. Professionals in the field are urged to
use research, play an ombudsman role on campus, emphasize
"PR" counseling, and do complete staff work. It also advises
professionals to keep confidences, work to advance their education,
understand the president's problems, learn about public opinion,
improve productivity, and evaluate performance. Individual
chapters discuss internal and external relations, news services,
broadcasting, special events, and photography for institutional
relations. (For a description of the *Handbook* in its entirety, see
entry number 54.)

136 Cole, Robert S. *The Practical Handbook of Public Relations.* Englewood Cliffs, N.J.: Prentice-Hall, 1982. 213
pages.

This manual discusses basic public relations techniques and
includes sample press kits and lead sentences for news releases,
with a list of public relations do's and don't's. The author focuses
on the role of the practitioner as a specialist in communications,
an analyst of public opinion, and a counselor to administrators.
The early chapters in this widely used textbook are especially
valuable, as they deal with functions, place, purpose, and process
of public relations. The book includes chapters on organizations

that practice public relations, including one in the field of higher education.

137 Council for Advancement and Support of Education. "New Technologies in Media Relations." *CASE Currents*, 1982, *8* (1), 12–18.

This special insert to *CASE Currents* contains three articles on using the new technologies of cable television and computers in media relations. The first two articles deal with cable television and its public relations potential; the last describes how a multiterminal computer system can help increase the productivity of a small news bureau.

138 Council for Advancement and Support of Education. *Communicating Science and Research.* Washington, D.C.: Council for Advancement and Support of Education, 1983. 13 pages.

Designed for the science writer, researcher, or editor, this publication includes material on placing science stories, descriptions of good research periodicals, information on how to edit science articles, and factors that the science writer should consider when working with researchers.

★**139** Cutlip, Scott M., Center, Allen H., and Broom, Glen M. *Effective Public Relations.* (6th ed.) Englewood Cliffs, N.J.: Prentice-Hall, 1985. 670 pages.

The most widely used textbook in the public relations field, this book offers the most comprehensive and up-to-date treatment of the subject of any work available. It was first published in 1952, and succeeding editions have kept its coverage of the field current with changes in the public relations field. The current edition prunes and completely updates the content to bring the text abreast of recent developments, points the way toward the future, and accurately reflects the rigor, precision, and growing emphasis on research that mark today's increasingly sophisticated professional leadership. The first part of this work, which treats principles and process, includes an introduction to contemporary public relations and chapters on how public relations evolved, practitioners of public relations, organizational content of public relations, the social context of public relations, and communication and public opinion. Chapters 9 through 12 do an excellent job of analyzing the process of public relations by defining public relations problems and exploring planning and programming, taking action and communicating, and evaluating programs. There are strong chapters on internal publics, internal communication media, and mass media, as well as on external publics, media relations, and the movement toward a profession. Part 2 of the book details the problems and practice in business, associations and professional societies, voluntary agencies, politics and government, and public schools and higher education. This work is also available in Italian, Japanese, Korean, and Spanish.

140 Grunig, James E., and Hunt, Todd. *Managing Public Relations.* New York: CBS Educational and Professional Publishing, 1983. 640 pages.

An instant reference to the skills and techniques used by public relations professionals, this practical guide is divided into four parts: "The Nature of Public Relations," "Principles of Public Relations Management," "Managing Public Relations Programs," and "Managing Public Relations Techniques." It provides models, surveys, and questionnaires to evaluate programs and uses case studies to illustrate points.

141 Lovell, Ronald P. *Inside Public Relations.* Newton, Mass.: Allyn & Bacon, 1982. 415 pages.

This basic textbook is divided into two major parts. The first provides a philosophical and informational base for public relations, covering such topics as the history of public relations, the various segments of the profession, and the determining of public relations goals. The second part describes the various techniques involved in developing public relations programs, explaining such tasks as writing news releases, preparing brochures and press kits, using advertisements, television, and radio, and setting up special events. It also covers how to deal with various publics, how to conduct public opinion surveys, and how to avoid legal and ethical problems.

★**142** Moore, R. Keith (ed.). *How to Make Big Improvements in Small PR Shops*. Washington, D.C.: Council for Advancement and Support of Education, 1985. 116 pages.

This publication contains sample policy statements, guidelines, job descriptions, and forms collected from sixteen colleges with small public relations staffs. Sample topics include crisis handling and suggestions to help faculty and staff respond to media inquiries.

★**143** Naisbitt, John. *Megatrends*. New York: Warner Books, 1984. 333 pages.

This best-seller examines the many ways in which America is restructuring, describing the ten new directions transforming our lives. These ten trends are of concern to the advancement professional. Practitioners of advancement do not function in a vacuum but in a vibrant and changing society. They never carry out their programs and activities apart from society; they must react and adapt to change. Thus, because the advancement practitioner must key his or her efforts to changes in society, this book becomes important in the identification of the ways that society is changing now and will change in the future. These trends will affect how the publics of our colleges and universities will understand and support them. *Megatrends* is a must for everyone who cares about tomorrow and who must function there.

★**144** Persons, Christopher Edgar. *Public Relations for Colleges and Universities: A Manual of Practical Procedure*. Stanford, Calif.: Stanford University Press, 1946. 61 pages.

In this still-relevant manual, the author defines and explains the administrator's position and function as they relate to public relations. The work provides a sound public relations procedure, covering such topics as the importance and foundation of public relations in colleges and universities, the setting of objectives, and overall organization and management of public relations activities.

★**145** Raley, Nancy S. (ed.). *Developing a Comprehensive PR Plan*. Washington, D.C.: Council for Advancement and Support of Education, 1978. (Microfiche.) 98 pages.

This microfiche contains both general guidance on how to develop comprehensive public relations plans and excerpts from the planning documents in use at various universities. It includes general discussions on such subjects as management and public relations by objectives and provides specific case-study examples from several institutions.

146 Reilly, Robert T. *Public Relations in Action*. Englewood Cliffs, N.J.: Prentice-Hall, 1981. 468 pages.

This textbook sets forth a practical course in public relations and provides information for ready application in a variety of settings. It describes how to write for various audiences, how to produce for the media, and how to evaluate public relations performance and examines the practice and applications of public relations in several organizations, including some in higher education.

147 Rowland, Howard Ray (ed.). "Part Two: Strengthening Institutional Relations." In A. Westley Rowland (gen. ed.), *Handbook of Institutional Advancement: A Practical Guide to College and University Relations, Fund Raising, Alumni Relations, Government Relations, Publications, and Executive Management for Continued Advancement.* (2nd ed.) San Francisco: Jossey-Bass, 1986. 99 pages.

This part of the *Handbook* examines the important advancement area of institutional relations, which encompasses general public relations, internal and external, and discusses how best to use the print and electronic media. The authors discuss the ideal characteristics of an institutional relations officer and stress methods for increasing professionalism, performance, and productivity. The latest methods and techniques involved in working with the media, both print and electronic, are discussed. Helpful information and checklists are provided for special events. Effective use of photographs in college and university publications is illustrated, and speech writing is discussed. (For a description of the *Handbook* in its entirety, see entry number 54.)

148 Schramm, Wilbur Lang, Roberts, Donald F., and Seitel, Fraser P. *The Practice of Public Relations.* (2nd ed.) Westerville, Ohio: Merrill, 1984. 545 pages.

This textbook combines the theory and practice of public relations in order to provide both the neophyte and the veteran with a comprehensive understanding of the field. It builds upon the central theme that public relations is a management process that is an integral part of the policy- and decision-making apparatus of any organization. Part 1 addresses the basics of public relations— what it is, how it is organized, and assorted research methods used. Part 2 examines such applications as writing, marketing, advertising, and support services and explores the various publics— employees, consumers, the government, and competitors. The book contains over sixty hypothetical and real-life case studies and interviews with twenty-three well-known public relations professionals.

149 Simon, Raymond. *Public Relations: Concepts and Practices.* (2nd ed.) Columbus, Ohio: Grid Publishing, 1980. 437 pages.

This textbook examines the essential nature of public relations, its role in American society, the practitioners who manage the function, and the dynamics of the public relations process. It covers such key areas as public opinion research, planning, programming, and communication feedback, using examples from a variety of nonprofit organizations (including higher education) as well as business and industry.

150 Sperber, Nathaniel N., and Lerbinger, Otto. *Manager's Public Relations Handbook*. Reading, Mass.: Addison-Wesley, 1982. 334 pages.

A practical book designed for corporate managers of public relations programs, most of this work also applies to the campus. Chapters deal with such topics as media relations, employee relations, special events, media exposure for the institution's executives, how to identify an institution's areas of vulnerability, and how to manage crises and disasters. It provides fifty-six checklists for anticipating, handling, and evaluating a variety of factors that can increase the effectiveness of the public relations program overall.

Effective Communication

151 Adler, Mortimer J. *How to Speak—How to Listen*. New York: Macmillan, 1983. 288 pages.

This book focuses on rules for effective delivery of what one has to say, for attentively and actively using one's mind in silent listening, and for making all varieties of two-way talk both more profitable and more pleasurable. The suggestions are especially applicable to all forms of persuasive speech.

152 Berlo, David K. *Process of Communication*. New York: Holt, Rinehart & Winston, 1960. 318 pages.

Stressing the way people communicate with each other, this classic book is concerned with the scope and purpose of communication, the factors involved in the process, and the role of language in human behavior. It describes people's behaviors and the relationships between the talker and the listener, the writer and the reader, the performer and the audience. It explores the complex nature of the communication process and the variety of factors affecting its results through early systems models and examples.

153 Bittner, John R. *Fundamentals of Communication.* Englewood Cliffs, N.J.: Prentice-Hall, 1985. 464 pages.

This comprehensive overview of the communication process blends the teaching of strong communication skills with contemporary underpinnings and incorporates numerous concrete examples from real-life settings. It aims at preparing students to be both responsible consumers and skilled practitioners of the art and science of human communication and covers all basic topics, including an enhanced section on public communication, with assorted learning aids and exercises.

★**154** Bittner, John R. *Mass Communication: An Introduction.* (4th ed.) Englewood Cliffs, N.J.: Prentice-Hall, 1986. 528 pages.

An excellent book for those who wish an up-to-date treatment of mass communication, this work considers print, film, and electronic mass media as well as the humanistic, artistic, and scientific approaches to mass communication. The chapter on "Mass Communication and New Technologies" incorporates everything in one place from cable television through satellites, interactive video, and electronic newspapers. A major chapter on ethics and social issues challenges the reader to think about the consequences of media's relationship to society. Separate chapters on advertising and public relations examine the inner workings of these media institutions. Additional chapters in the book discuss the nature of mass communication, newspapers, magazines, book publishing, radio, television, photography and photojournalism, motion pictures, the recording industry, advertising, computers and data processing in mass communication and legal issues and the working press.

155 Black, Jay, and Whitney, Fredrick C. *Introduction to Mass Communication.* Dubuque, Iowa: Brown, 1983. 472 pages.

This book analyzes the mass communication empires of print, electronic, and persuasive media. Each one is examined in light of its historical development, its relationship to other media, its affect on audiences, its probable future, and its broad social functions and individual characteristics. The book also examines controls on mass media: the law, government regulations, social responsibility, and media ethics. It includes a glossary and bibliography.

156 Council for Advancement and Support of Education. *How to Improve Your Writing.* Washington, D.C.: Council for Advancement and Support of Education, 1983. 11 pages.

This publication includes techniques for clear, effective writing; suggestions for nonsexist language; a list of misused and overused words; and tips on better communication through simple, direct language.

★**157** Flesch, Rudolf. *The Art of Readable Writing.* New York: Harper & Row, 1949. 237 pages.

A practical complement to Flesch's previous book, *The Art of Plain Talk,* this book describes how to write in clear and simple ways that increase understandability and readability. Using a revised readability formula, Flesch puts a premium on techniques that avoid confusion. The book itself is an excellent example of readable writing.

158 Gayley, Henry. *How to Write for Development.* Washington, D.C.: Council for Advancement and Support of Education, 1981. 350 pages.

This book offers step-by-step guidelines for writing proposals, annual reports, case statements, fund-raising brochures, and letters. It also explains factors to be considered prior to writing, including appealing to readers and presenting your message.

★**159** Goldhaber, Gerald M. (ed.). *Improving Institutional Communication.* New Directions for Institutional Advancement, no. 2. San Francisco: Jossey-Bass, 1978. 99 pages.

This book deals with the most important process in any organization. It identifies the variables that are most central to both internal and external communication systems and presents detailed plans to help institutions assess the effectiveness of their communications systems and specific recommendations to both strengthen and improve them.

★**160** Goldhaber, Gerald M. *Organizational Communication.* (3rd ed.) Dubuque, Iowa: Brown, 1983. 510 pages.

This book focuses on the essential nature of communication in organizations, defining the nature of this communication and explaining the theory of organization and organizational communication climate. Important for the advancement professional are chapters on the process of communication, the interaction formats of organizational communication, small-group organizational communication, public organizational communication, and organizational communication diagnosis and change.

161 Goldhaber, Gerald M., Dennis, Harry, S., III, Richetto, Gary M., and Wiio, Osmo. *Information Strategies: New Pathways to Management Productivity.* (Rev. ed.) Norwood, N.J.: Ablex, 1984. 366 pages.

Written for managers, supervisors, and leaders of any type of organization, this book aims at improving the ability to communicate in order to achieve optimal power in the organization. The book provides an overview of information power theory (the key external and internal contingencies affecting an organization's information system), presents the major personal, relational, and organizational communication variables that constitute an organization's information system, and offers a variety of tools and methods that can be used to assess an organization's communication system. Updated versions of useful communication-audit instruments are provided, including the first U.S. publication of the revised version of the classic organizational communication development (OCD) survey. The appendix includes descriptions of current research findings and reflections on the state of organizational communication research.

162 Hiebert, Ray Eldon, Ungurart, Donald F., and Bohn, Thomas W. *Mass Media: An Introduction to Modern Communications.* New York: McKay, 1975. 494 pages.

This book introduces the reader to the grammar of the mass media as we now know it. It approaches mass communication as a process, describing the component parts as well as the media themselves, the uses to which they are put, and the effect they have on society. It surveys all the mass media systems and establishes a theoretical base, while discussing the practical aspects of communications. It contains an annotated bibliography.

163 Roman, Kenneth, and Raphaelson, Joel. *Writing That Works.* New York: Harper & Row, 1981. 160 pages.

An easy-to-read and practical book on good writing that is particularly applicable to the needs of fund raisers, this book begins with the principles of effective writing and then goes on to show how to write with clarity, precision, brevity, and the force of logic. It provides dozens of comparisons, including examples of good and bad writing for fund raising, and shows how to apply the principles of good writing to letters, memos, fund-raising appeals, speeches, and reports.

164 Smeltzer, Larry R., and Waltman, John L. *Managerial Communication: A Strategic Approach.* New York: Wiley, 1984. 556 pages.

This book is designed to help develop professional strategic communications by providing the reader with knowledge in the field of managerial communications and with the skills needed to develop solutions to communication problems. Strategies are provided for written and oral managerial communications and for such specialized applications as technologically mediated managerial communications. It draws heavily on the use of case studies, many written by practicing managers. Appendixes include a discussion of the legal dimensions of managerial communications, a sample of report forms to use in conducting a case study, and a glossary.

165 Tompkins, Phillip K. *Communication as Action: An Introduction to Rhetoric and Communication.* Belmont, Calif.: Wadsworth, 1982. 253 pages.

This is an introductory text on rhetoric and communication with the threefold purpose of helping the reader acquire communications skills, gain an increased appreciation of achievement in theory and practice, and develop the ability to detect misuses of rhetoric and communication. The book reviews the foundations of rhetoric and communication and examines both micro and macro communication settings.

166 Verderber, Rudolph C. *Communicate.* (2nd ed.) Belmont, Calif.: Wadsworth, 1978. 381 pages.

This textbook covers personal communication, small-group communication, and public speaking. It includes many examples and provides useful exercises. The chapters on public speaking cover such topics as preparing the speech, principles of persuasion, delivering the speech, and choosing speeches for special occasions.

Internal Relations

★167 Bonus, Thaddeus. *Improving Internal Communication.* Washington, D.C.: Council for Advancement and Support of Education, 1983. 130 pages.

This is an important work for advancement people who are concerned with improving internal communication at their institutions. It deals with the flow of information through every channel on campus, such as from supervisor to employees and from the president's office to the grounds crew. It describes how to develop an internal communication plan, use research to evaluate communication needs, write and edit for the internal audience, and communicate effectively through several mediums, elaborating on internal communication staff size and budget, major periodical frequency, and audience and distribution. An interesting feature in the appendix is a valuable instrument for comparing one's program with others, which is used to describe an internal communication matrix of programs in place at eighty institutions.

★**168** Council for Advancement and Support of Education. "Internal Communications." *CASE Currents*, 1977, *2* (entire issue 10).

This special issue of *CASE Currents* focuses on how to communicate successfully with the internal publics of a college or university—faculty, administrators, staff, and students. Various authors discuss the use of research, the problems posed by crisis situations, such as strikes, and the ways in which good internal communication improves campus morale and reduces staff turnover. The issue summarizes some of the best internal newsletters and newspapers from colleges and universities in the country.

External Relations

169 Balthaser, William. *Publicity Portfolio.* (4th ed.) Ambler, Pa.: Fund-Raising Institute, 1978. 58 pages.

This book presents techniques for supporting fund raising with attention-getting publicity. It explains that good publicity is that which sends the right material, in the right form, to the right person, at the right time and tells how to draft publicity programs, how to prepare such items as news releases, captions, radio releases, and memos to editors, and how to manage publicity programs. It contains a one-page publicity checklist and many illustrations and samples.

170 Benezet, Louis T., and Magnusson, Frances W. (eds.). *Building Bridges to the Public.* New Directions for Higher Education, no. 27. San Francisco: Jossey-Bass, 1979. 104 pages.

This book provides an overview of why higher education needs more public understanding and how to build that understanding. Several authors describe how their colleges and universities have developed academic and service programs that contribute to the public interest and build public support for the institution. A chapter by Harvey Jacobson outlines the factors that inhibit and foster good communication.

★**171** Council for Advancement and Support of Education. "Community Relations." *CASE Currents,* 1978, *4* (entire issue 5).

This issue explores the topic of effective community relations. The first article suggests two dozen ways to keep community relations blooming; others focus on cultivating one's "backyard," turning foes to friends, sharing the institution's mission, putting research to use, and "sewing the gown to the town." This is must reading for those interested in effective community relations.

172 Farlow, Helen. *Publicizing and Promoting Programs.* New York: McGraw-Hill, 1979. 277 pages.

Directed at those who engage in publicizing continuing education in colleges as well as other institutions, this manual provides examples of publicity methods used for a variety of programs and purposes. It includes a glossary and annotated bibliography.

173 Hendrickson, Gayle A. *Promoting Continuing Education.* Washington, D.C.: Council for Advancement and Support of Education, 1980. 61 pages.

This publication presents ways to identify target audiences and select the appropriate promotional strategies to reach them. The section on external direct-mail publications deals with planning, printing, and mailing schedules, organizing contents, and designing publicity materials and includes advice on selecting mailing lists. The final chapter describes how to analyze current promotional strategies and identify areas for improvement.

★**174** Rowland, Howard Ray (ed.). *Effective Community Relations.* New Directions for Institutional Advancement, no. 10. San Francisco: Jossey-Bass, 1980. 120 pages.

This sourcebook explains why community support is needed now more than ever and describes how to develop mutually beneficial "town-gown" relations. It demonstrates how institutions can help meet community needs, share their resources, and project themselves into the community and includes case studies of programs at various leading institutions.

175 Winkler, H. Donald. "Backyard Diplomacy." *CASE Currents,* 1984, *10* (8), 34–38.

The major thesis of this excellent article on community relations, of value to all advancement professionals, is that good community relations begin at home, and the advancement professional should try to establish links with target groups and leaders in the community. Winkler suggests two ways to bring about mutual understanding and appreciation: establishing two-way communication with targeted groups and leaders and building public appreciation through projects that meet community needs. He advises advancement practitioners to seek out the people in the community who want to be friends and help them to provide support; remember that good citizenship begins at home; concentrate more on what the audience wants to know and less on what the institution wants to say; be concerned about impressions and experiences of campus visitors; and centralize all communication to external publics.

Print Media

176 Berger, Joel S. (ed.). *Making Your News Service More Effective.* (3rd ed.) Washington, D.C.: Council for Advancement and Support of Education, 1981. 227 pages.

This loose-leaf handbook explores forty-six aspects of news services, including managing the news bureau, computerized news releases, writing science and feature copy, dealing with crisis situations, the small shop, and how to work with radio and television.

★**177** Ciervo, Arthur V. (ed.). *Using the Mass Media.* New Directions for Institutional Advancement, no. 5. San Francisco: Jossey-Bass, 1979. 90 pages.

This sourcebook explains how colleges and universities can increase and improve the information about their purposes, plans, and programs in the print media, television, and radio. Every aspect of media usage, from tailoring stories for specific audiences to evaluating the entire communications program of the institution, is discussed.

178 Desruisseaux, Paul. "The Ps and Qs of Q and A." *CASE Currents,* 1984, *10,* 50–52.

This article explores effective interviewing, a craft that must be practiced by many advancement professionals. Desruisseaux says that the most important part of interviewing is getting people to talk; to do this, he suggests preparing for an interview with the same type of research as would be done for any other story. Once the subject is talking, the interviewer must carefully listen, helping the talkative person to get to the point. Other suggestions he offers include getting details, taking good notes, recontacting subjects, and limiting interview sessions to no longer than two hours.

★**179** *Editor and Publisher Yearbook.* New York: Editor and Publisher Magazine, 1985.

Published annually, this is an encyclopedia of the newspaper industry. It covers listings of newspapers, syndicated services, mechanical equipment, organizations, and industry services in the United States and elsewhere. It includes more than 250,000 facts about newspapers and is a must for all advancement practitioners who deal with the print media.

★**180** IMS. *Ayer Directory of Publications.* Bala Cynwyd, Pa.: 1985. 1,400 pages.

The professional's directory of print media, this work is published annually. An alphabetical index provides the reader access to more than 900 classifications, including daily and weekly newspapers and magazines, such as consumer, business, technical, professional, trade, and farm publications. Names of editors, circulation, frequency, and related data are also provided.

181 IMS Press. *East Coast Publicity Directory.* Fort Washington, Pa.: IMS Press, 1984. 300 pages.

This comprehensive guide features in-depth information on newspapers, periodicals, radio, television, cable, and other communication services (news/wire services, feature syndicates, and so on). Each entry provides address and telephone number, circulation/audience, subscription rates, type of medium, primary contents, and editorial staff. It covers all the major East Coast markets and includes 200 national listings as well.

182 Jacobi, Peter. *Writing with Style: The News Story and the Feature.* Chicago: Lawrence Ragan Communications, 1983. 111 pages.

This book not only describes good writing but also provides a wealth of examples. At least half of the text is devoted to examples of well-written features and news stories from all kinds of publications.

★**183** National Research Bureau. *1985 Working Press of the Nation.* 5 vols. Chicago: National Research Bureau, 1984.

This five-volume media directory lists newspapers, magazines, television and radio stations, feature writers and photographers, and assorted internal publications. Each volume contains standardized entries with general information such as address, telephone number, circulation, rates, publication frequency, area served, network affiliation, current personnel (editors, executives, owners, managers, and bureau contacts), deadlines by nature of story and material submitted, and information on the kinds of material accepted. Indexes to the individual volumes provide quick access to information.

★**184** Raley, Nancy S. (ed.). *Updating Your News Service.* Washington, D.C.: Council for Advancement and Support of Education, 1980. 194 pages plus eight tapes.

This CASE audio-print career development kit includes eight tapes on news and information techniques and current technology and a handbook, *Making Your News Service More Effective,* edited by Joel S. Berger (see entry number 176). Tapes cover launching a low-budget radio operation, writing broadcast copy, getting television coverage without production facilities, producing effective radio-television public-service announcements, getting coverage without releases, and handling hometown stories.

Electronic Media

185 Becker, William B. *TV News Handbook.* (2nd ed.) Southfield, Mich.: Insiders Guide, 1982. 110 pages.

This collection of helpful hints for those dealing with television news is recommended for the beginner.

186 Larimi Communications Associates. *Cable Contacts Yearbook*. New York: Larimi Communications Associates, 1985. 400 pages.

This new directory lists over 450 cable systems in major markets throughout the United States, including satellite networks, independent producers, news services, and multiple-system operators. Local cable-system listings include data-channel information, public-access channel descriptions, local-origination programming, subscribers served, and contact persons. Independently produced programs are indexed by network and producer, with information on technical and visual support requirements, subscriber figures, and preproduced segment or joint-production opportunities.

187 Larimi Communications Associates. *Radio Contacts*. New York: Larimi Communications Associates, 1985. 1,300 pages.

This yearly directory of local network and syndicated radio programming throughout the United States lists 4,000 major-market stations, providing data on network affiliation, news services, personnel, program format, guest and information requirements, booking times, and contact persons. It is updated monthly, with daily updating service available.

188 Larimi Communications Associates. *Television Contacts*. New York: Larimi Communications Associates, 1985. 550 pages.

This is a yearly directory of national, syndicated, and local television news, "talk," and public affairs programs in the United States and major Canadian markets. Listings include address, personnel, network affiliation, contact person, audience figures when available, guest information, and placement information. It is updated monthly.

189 Larimi Communications Associates. *TV News*. New York: Larimi Communications Associates, 1985. 500 pages.

This is a yearly guide to news directors, assignment editors, and news programs of local television stations and networks in the United States and Canada. Subject listings describe guest usage, information requirements, and specialist reporter or contact person. Network listings include bureau chiefs, addresses, and program listings.

190 Miller, Nancy Huber. "Radioactivity." *CASE Currents*, 1984, *10* (3), 10–13.

The author of this article stresses that radio has grown in importance, with more stations, more diverse markets, and a bigger target audience than ever before. She describes special programs developed for radio by Pennsylvania State University and encourages advancement practitioners to recognize the implications of radio, analyze its cost advantages, realize its limitations, and adapt copy for radio use.

191 Raley, Nancy. "A Medley of Radio Winners." *CASE Currents*, 1984, *10* (3), 18–23.

This article consists of short excerpts from radio spots prepared by advancement professionals. It covers news services, radio series, paid advertising, and public-service announcements.

192 Zehring, John William. "Good Vibrations." *CASE Currents*, 1984, *10* (5), 14–16.

The author of this article stresses the importance of radio and makes a case for its use by colleges and universities: more people get their first morning news from radio than from any other source; radio news stories often air between six and twenty-four times a day; any radio news has the impact of front-page news; radio reaches a higher percentage of affluent consumers than do other media; and 99 percent of American homes, as well as 95 percent of all new cars, are equipped with radios. Zehring discusses the use of actualities and what the basic setup includes. To produce a good radio news story, he suggests that one start with the institution's name; give more information than is needed; write for the ear, not the eye; analyze local newscasts; use two actualities when desirable; and write a story so that it demands to be heard.

Special Events

★**193** Council for Advancement and Support of Education. "Special Events." *CASE Currents,* 1980, *6* (entire issue 6).

This issue of *CASE Currents* includes "how-to" articles and a number of special-events case studies. The lead article outlines the importance of matching events with goals; it discusses goals, themes, and audiences and lists ten elements for success. The last article—"How to Sleep at Night: Check it Out"—provides a checklist for ensuring that the special event is carried out successfully. Five basic planning steps are suggested: identify the audience, define goals, understand the product, break the boredom barrier, and innovate to stay fresh. The comprehensive checklist covers advance planning, invitations and seating, housing, transportation, general operations, dignitaries, security, receptions and meals, a rain plan, registration, speakers, advance promotion, special publications, and a total information plan. This excellent series of articles is of special value to anyone involved in planning any type of a special event.

194 Council for Advancement and Support of Education. "Inaugurations." *CASE Currents,* 1984, *10* (entire issue 5).

This special issue of *CASE Currents* focuses on the in's and out's of staging presidential inaugurations. It covers planning, developing inaugural publications, and avoiding protocol pitfalls and includes a time line for planning inaugural activities.

195 Council for Advancement and Support of Education. "Anniversaries." *CASE Currents,* 1984, *10* (entire issue 6).

This issue of *CASE Currents,* which focuses on institutional anniversaries, describes how an anniversary observance can attract media coverage, involve alumni, and raise funds. It explains how to publish the institution's history, how to involve volunteers in planning and staging the anniversary festivities.

196 Leibert, Edwin R., and Sheldon, Bernice, E. *Handbook of Special Events for Nonprofit Organizations*. Chicago: Association Press, 1974. 224 pages.

This publication offers useful guidance on staging special events. Separate sections cover public relations/cultivation and fundraising events. It includes a compilation of ideas for special occasions.

197 Sheerin, Mira. *How to Raise Top Dollars from Special Events*. Hartsdale, N.Y.: Public Service Materials Center, 1984. 123 pages.

This encyclopedic guide to successful special events of every type—art exhibits and previews, sporting events, gala performances, open-house tours, block parties, antique shows, bazaars, telethons, auctions, tournaments, balls, tribute dinners and luncheons, and many more—explains how to select the right event, what ten elements must be included in all events, how to stay within budget, and how to deal with the unexpected. It includes samples of press releases, invitations, thank-yous, programs, and provides information on increasing income through souvenir journals and raffles.

198 Wyatt, Joan Lynott. *The "How-To" Book*. Tacoma, Wash.: Office of Public Relations, University of Puget Sound, 1978. 49 pages.

This is a practical guide on how to plan and carry out successful college and university special events. Drawing on strong campus experience, the author covers topics such as getting clearance for the events, scheduling timetables, staffing, booking facilities, budgeting, planning food functions, arranging auxiliary events, audiovisual needs, traffic and parking, emergency information and security, and follow-up. She also discusses publications and media coverage for enhancing the special event.

Speech Writing

199 Arnold, Edmund, and Tarver, Jerry (eds.). *Speechwriters Newsletter*. Chicago: Lawrence Ragan Communications, 1985. Variable pages.

This weekly guide elaborates on specific techniques, how-to-do-it information, and case histories that can serve as a useful source for speech writers in all topic areas.

200 Burson-Marsteller. *The Executive Speechmaker: A Systems Approach*. New York: Foundation for Public Relations Research and Education, 1980. 43 pages.

A guidebook on speech writing and speechmaking designed for executives and managers, this work includes information on how to organize a speechmaking system, how to develop specific skills, and how to get the most from an investment. It contains practical advice on such important steps as setting objectives, choosing speech platforms, and the pros and cons of panel appearances. Three useful checklists are provided.

201 Tarver, Jerry. *Professional Speech Writing*. Richmond, Va.: Effective Speech Writing Institute, University of Richmond, 1982. 200 pages.

This book provides an excellent insight into what the business of speech writing is all about. Based on twenty years of teaching and consulting, it includes the history and status of speech writing, speaker-writer relationships, audience analysis and speech objectives, organization of ideas, use of evidence, oral style, effective humor, presenting the speech, and special types of speeches.

202 Welsh, James J. *The Speech Writing Guide.* New York: Wiley, 1968. 128 pages.

This publication provides a guide for professionals who are regular speakers as well as those who are required to make only an occasional speech. A practical reference tool for writing an effective speech, it covers topics such as clarity, unity, economy of words, choice of subjects, and principles of speech delivery.

Photography

203 Council for Advancement and Support of Education. "Focus on Photography." *CASE Currents,* 1984, *10* (4), 8-17.

This special section offers suggestions for bringing your publication's photography to life, such as being alert to unusual situations, understanding the event being photographed, blurring the background, capturing relationships, going behind the scene for some special photos, getting close to subjects, moving around, and trying to capture the humor in a situation.

204 Douglas, Philip N. *Pictures for Organizations: How and Why They Work as Communication.* Chicago: Lawrence Ragan Communications, 1982. 234 pages.

Discussing over 100 examples, the author explores how specific photographs work as communication in the editorial media of organizations. The book is intended to help photographers and editors recognize the concepts, techniques, and stylistic approaches that make the difference between an effective photograph and an ineffective one.

4

Fund Raising

The oldest of the advancement functions is fund raising, which began with the establishment of Harvard University. Since that time, it has, in various forms, been an indispensable element in the resource-development program of every college and university. In a recent survey, it was found that fund raising is the predominant responsibility of CASE member representatives, with more than one-third saying they work on the development or fund-raising staff of an educational institution. During the 1980s, fund raising has assumed an even more important role in colleges and universities, as all institutions face a financial crunch because of reduced enrollments, the state of the economy, demographic changes, competition for state funds, and a withdrawal of support by the federal government from many programs.

The sources of support for all of higher education have become blurred. No longer does the private institution depend exclusively on its private benefactors and tuition; in many states, public funds are made available to support private higher education. In turn, because of the heavy demands on the states' resources (welfare, transportation, health, public safety, and law enforcement), the public colleges and universities of the nation have turned to private sources of support to supplement their state allocations—not, as in the past, to provide them with the "margin of greatness" or the "extras for excellence" but, in fact, to provide for some of their urgent operating and capital needs. It is still true, however, that private funds make a vital difference between whether a state university is "average" or "great"; every "great" state university depends on private funds for an important share of its total budget. Private funds meet needs that the state cannot be expected to finance, such as scholarships and fellowships, special research and teaching equipment, experimental educational programs, athletic programs, funds for distinguished scholars, specialized library acquisitions, student-faculty loans, grants for research projects (especially seed money), support for conferences and seminars, support for off-campus projects, faculty awards, and international travel.

All fund-raising efforts of colleges and universities appeal to the idea of philanthropy, a uniquely American concept. Americans give for many reasons: concern for humanity, tax considerations, religion, gratitude for services, perpetuation of personal ideals, values, and goals through an institution, societal pressures, and even fear or guilt. In 1984, more than 230 million Americans made contributions to over 300,000 charitable groups; the total sum given was $74.25 billion, an amount greater than the national budgets of two-thirds of the world's countries. The sources and recipients of these contributions are shown in Table 1. Of the total philanthropy, $5.60 billion was given to higher education, an increase of 8.5 percent over the amount given the previous year. Table 2 shows the sources of these contributions.

Development requires an honest appraisal of the institution and its prospects, together with a realistic awareness that alumni, corporations, foundations, and governmental agencies are not simply standing around waiting to shower colleges and universities with money. Successful fund raising requires the craft of selling a profitable investment to those who can and want to buy and the expertise to match the need with the potential donor. Common elements in an effective development program include a strong case for support, coordination among all the areas of advancement, presidential leadership and participation, special recognition of major contributors, committed volunteers with appropriate staff support, and regular communication with potential and actual contributors, including expressions of appreciation to donors and reports of how their contributions are being used. The literature annotated in this chapter discusses ways to develop these elements in a variety of fund-raising applications—the annual fund, deferred giving and estate planning, corporate giving, foundation giving, and capital campaigns.

**Table 1. Total U.S. Charitable Contributions, 1984
(in Billions of Dollars).**

	Amount	Percentage of Total
Sources		
Individuals	$61.55	82.9
Bequests	4.89	6.6
Foundations	4.36	5.8
Corporations	3.45	4.7
Recipients		
Religious groups	35.56	47.9
Health care and hospitals	10.44	14.1
Education	10.08	13.6
Social welfare	8.01	10.8
Arts and humanities	4.64	6.2
Civic and public organizations	2.08	2.8
Other	3.44	4.6

Source: American Association of Fund-Raising Counsel. *Giving USA: Annual Report 1985.* New York: American Association of Fund-Raising Counsel, 1985.

**Table 2. U.S. Charitable Contributions to
Higher Education, 1984
(in Millions of Dollars).**

Source	Amount
Alumni	$1,305
Other individuals	1,316
Corporations	1,271
Foundations	1,081
Religious groups	190
Other	437

Source: American Association of Fund-Raising Counsel. *Giving USA: Annual Report 1985.* New York: American Association of Fund-Raising Counsel, 1985.

General

205 Alberger, Patricia L. (ed.). *Winning Techniques for Athletic Fund Raising*. Washington, D.C.: Council for Advancement and Support of Education, 1981. 97 pages.

Successful fund raisers explain how they organize campaigns and volunteers, take their programs on the road, involve coaches and athletic directors, and utilize the funds they raise. The work includes advice on donor recognition and perquisites, major-gift clubs, and campaign timetables. Experts also discuss specific fund-raising techniques for women's athletics.

★206 American Association of Fund-Raising Counsel. *Giving U.S.A.: A Compilation of Facts and Trends on American Philanthropy for the Year 1984*. (30th annual issue) American Association of Fund-Raising Counsel, 1985. 113 pages.

This annual publication provides information on who gives, how much is given, and for what purposes contributions are made. The narrative accompanying the data provides a useful overview of philanthropy and philanthropical trends. The data are presented within the categories of philanthropical source (individual, bequest, foundations, and corporations) and particular activity (education, health, art, and culture).

207 American Association of State Colleges and Universities. *Proposal Development Handbook*. (Rev. ed.) Washington, D.C.: Office of Federal Programs, American Association of State Colleges and Universities, 1982. 12 pages.

A brief but comprehensive review of the essential concepts involved in proposal writing, this brochure is designed to supplement official agency and foundation guidelines.

208 American Council on Education. *The Complete Grants Sourcebook for Higher Education*. New York: Macmillan, 1980. 605 pages.

Designed specifically for colleges and universities, this guide provides detailed information on more than 500 foundations, corporations, and federal programs. Agency entries include programs of interest, eligibility requirements and policies, financial profile, contact persons, and a selection of past awards. The book also serves as a guide to applying for grants, with practical advice on finding sources, writing proposals, and securing continued support. It includes checklists, sample inquiries, proposals, and budgets.

209 Arnove, Robert F. (ed.). *Philanthropy and Cultural Imperialism*. Boston: Holland, 1980. 473 pages.

In this work, intended as a sourcebook on the origins, workings, and consequences of modern philanthropical foundations, critical articles examine the activities of foundations in the production of culture and the formation of public policy. The book offers a variety of ideological perspectives centering around the ways three principal foundations function in American society and the concentration of wealth and power that helps maintain an economic and political order.

210 Berendt, Robert J., and Taft, J. Richard. *How to Rate Your Development Office: A Fund-Raising Primer for the Chief Executive*. Washington, D.C.: Taft Corporation, 1983. 88 pages.

A guidebook covering all the specific details that chief executives or board members should be looking for when evaluating the development office, this book will also help professional development officers assess, analyze, and evaluate the development program.

211 Brakeley, George A., Jr. *Tested Ways to Successful Fund Raising*. Hartsdale, N.Y.: Public Service Materials Center, 1984. 116 pages.

Brakeley, a veteran professional in the fund-raising field, shares many of his professional secrets in this book, which covers all forms of fund raising, including direct mail, deferred giving, annual campaigns, capital campaigns, corporate and foundation solicitation, and special events. It includes Brakeley's "Nine Key Factors in Motivating Donors."

★**212** Broce, Thomas E. *Fund Raising: The Guide to Raising Money from Private Sources*. Norman: University of Oklahoma Press, 1979. 254 pages.

Broce provides specific guidance on how to design and implement a successful fund-raising program, with a step-by-step approach to getting annual gifts and foundation and corporate support, running a capital campaign, and identifying, evaluating, and soliciting prospects. Appendixes include useful models for case statements, inquiry letters, and formal proposals, as well as samples of organization and flowcharts, time schedules, and a detailed action outline.

213 Cheshire, Richard D. (ed.). "Part Two: Fund Raising." In A. Westley Rowland (gen. ed.), *Handbook of Institutional Advancement: A Practical Guide to College and University Relations, Fund Raising, Alumni Relations, Government Relations, Publications, and Executive Management for Continued Advancement*. (1st ed.) San Francisco: Jossey-Bass, 1977. 154 pages.

This part of the *Handbook* is devoted to the nature, types, and importance of fund raising in colleges and universities, including discussions of the management of volunteers and the future of educational fund raising. (For a description of the *Handbook* in its entirety, see entry number 54.) Part 2 explains how fund raising makes possible a margin of educational difference in both public and private institutions, making colleges and universities better, more accessible, and more independent.

214 Conrad, Daniel Lynn. *How to Solicit Big Gifts.* San Francisco: Public Management Institute, 1978. 250 pages.

This comprehensive and practical manual offers help in developing the skills needed for effective face-to-face fund-raising ventures, with details on setting up training programs for staff and volunteers in capital campaigns, annual-fund drives, and major-gift solicitations. Topics include how to locate prospects, how to find and train solicitors, how to determine prospect giving potentials, twenty-eight ways to overcome prospect objections, how to phrase a request for a big gift, and follow-up techniques to ensure repeated giving.

215 Conrad, Daniel Lynn. *The Quick Proposal Workbook.* San Francisco: Public Management Institute, 1980. 119 pages.

This step-by-step approach to proposal writing explains how to eliminate ambiguity and clutter from your writing to express the proposal in a straightforward, compelling fashion. Topics cover developing proposal ideas, formulating ideas into projects, constructing proposals, plotting time lines for each activity of the project, determining needs at each phase, and developing a budget.

216 Council for Advancement and Support of Education. "Direct Mail." *CASE Currents,* 1978, *4* (entire issue 5).

The ten articles included in this special issue of *CASE Currents* offer tips for conducting direct-mail campaigns, including how to write letters that sell, how to use direct mail to reach students, the necessity of advance planning in direct-mail campaigns, and the ABC's of fund raising by mail.

217 Council for Advancement and Support of Education. "The Big Gift." *CASE Currents*, 1982, *8* (entire issue 4).

This special issue of *CASE Currents* presents several practical articles on how to cultivate big gifts, how to call on a prospect, and when, why, and how to ask for a contribution. It also includes a volunteer's guide to asking for a major gift, profiles of seven big givers and askers, and a discussion on the continuing debate over the role of the chief development officer in the "big gifts" game.

218 Council for Advancement and Support of Education. "Institutionally Related Foundations." *CASE Currents*, 1983, *9* (2), 40–51.

This special insert offers help in determining a foundation's degree of independence, working with legal considerations, drafting a charter, setting operating policies, and revitalizing a passive foundation.

219 Council for Advancement and Support of Education and National Council of University Business Officers. *Management Reporting Standards for Educational Institutions: Fund Raising and Related Activities*. Washington, D.C.: Council for Advancement and Support of Education, 1983. 18 pages.

This manual provides a set of definitions for management reporting standards for fund raising and related activities that will encourage college and university development professionals to "speak the same language." Definitions conform to the requirements of part 5 of the College and University Business Administration guide and the AICPA guide, *Audits of Colleges and Universities,* as amended. It also provides sample report forms and worksheets.

★**220** Council for Financial Aid to Education. *1983–84 Voluntary Support of Education.* New York: Council for Financial Aid to Education, 1985. 73 pages.

This volume reports on the support received during 1982–83 by 1,137 colleges and universities and 480 independent schools that responded to a CFAE survey. The survey results describe the statistics for twenty-one basic giving categories, plus educational expenditures and market value of endowments for each of the responding institutions. This report makes it possible for institutions to compare themselves with other similar institutions. The publication identifies which institutions receive what amount, for what purposes, and from whom.

★**221** Curti, Merle, and Nash, Roderic. *Philanthropy in Shaping of Higher Education.* New Brunswick, N.J.: Rutgers University Press, 1965. 340 pages.

In this history of philanthropy to American higher education, the authors examine both the positive and negative aspects of philanthropy on campus, chronicling how it has shaped educational policies, ideas, and theories, how it provided the necessary funds for expansion, and how it helped to establish standards of quality. The work provides an insightful perspective on the history of philanthropy, of higher education, and of the relationships among philanthropists, institutions of philanthropy, and institutions of higher education. Alumni, foundations, and corporations are given special attention.

222 Dermer, Joseph (ed.). *America's Most Successful Fund Raising Letters.* Hartsdale, N.Y.: Public Service Materials Center, 1976. 256 pages.

This work presents a collection of sixty-seven appeal letters that were winners in a nationwide contest sponsored by Public Service Materials Center. The letters cover a wide variety of fund-raising situations, including thank-yous, securing attendance at special events, gaining support from business leaders, securing bequests, and seeking volunteers. The letter writers also provide information on the objectives and results of each campaign represented. Forty-four pages of sample letters from colleges and universities are also included.

★**223** Faust, Paula (ed.). *An Introduction to Fund Raising: The Newcomer's Guide to Development.* Washington, D.C.: Council for Advancement and Support of Education, 1983. 92 pages.

This overview of the theories behind development, including various positions on the advancement program and personal qualities that lead to professional success, covers the basics on annual giving, the capital campaign, deferred giving, corporate and foundation support, research and record keeping, and computer applications for development. A fine book for beginners, this is also a useful reference for veterans.

★**224** Filer, John. *Giving in America: Toward a Stronger Voluntary Sector.* New York: Commission on Private Philanthropy and Public Needs, 1975. 240 pages.

Also known as the "Filer report," this work reports the findings and recommendations of the Commission on Private Philanthropy and Public Needs resulting from years of research and discussion over the roles of philanthropical giving and the voluntary (third) sector. It discusses ways in which the third sector and the practice of private giving can be strengthened and made more effective. The recommendations fall into three categories: proposals involving taxes and giving; proposals that seek to improve the philanthropical process; and a proposal to establish a permanent commission on the third sector.

225 The Fund-Raising Institute. *Fund-Raising by Computer.* Ambler, Pa.: Fund-Raising Institute, 1977. 135 pages.

This jargon-free guide to evaluating computer-generated fund-raising services includes a glossary, a consumer's guide to computer service bureaus, and information on selection costs. It provides a step-by-step account of how one organization successfully switched to an in-house computer system within eighteen months, with increases in efficiency but not in staff. Case studies from such colleges and universities as Brown, Yale, and the University of Nebraska are also included.

226 Harrison, Randall P. *Fund Raising by Formula: Steps to Make People Give.* Hartsdale, N.Y.: Public Service Materials Center, 1984. 112 pages.

Written by a research psychologist, this book explains why people and organizations give and provides a step-by-step formula for increasing levels of support. Topics cover securing contributions from new prospects; enlisting volunteers; direct-mail and telephone solicitations; obtaining grants from corporations, foundations, and government; bequests; and special events.

★**227** Heemann, Warren (ed.). *Analyzing the Cost Effectiveness of Fund Raising.* New Directions for Institutional Advancement, no. 3. San Francisco: Jossey-Bass, 1979. 90 pages.

This sourcebook presents an in-depth analysis of the costs and revenues of many of the country's most successful advancement programs and proposes methods of determining the actual costs of fund-raising programs in order to evaluate program productivity in relation to cost.

228 Hickey, James, and Koochoo, Elizabeth. *Prospecting: Searching Out the Philanthropic Dollar.* (2nd ed.) Washington, D.C.: Taft Corporation, 1984. 70 pages plus forms kit.

Starting with the assumption that nothing is as important as identifying and evaluating potential contributors, this book is aimed at helping in establishing and improving prospect procedures at an institution. It covers all major aspects of prospect research, including collecting research materials, keeping records, assessing donor potential, and analyzing trends and gift patterns.

A forms kit includes sample donor-record forms, prospect-record forms, individual- and corporate-donor fact sheets, and more.

229 Hodgson, Richard. *Direct Mail and Mail Order Handbook.* (3rd ed.) Chicago: Dartnell, 1980. 1,538 pages.

An all-inclusive manual that discusses every kind of sale promotion, advertising device, and selling technique, this work covers the basics of direct mail from formats, wages, and controls to fund raising, promotional services, campaign planning, and market research and is of particular interest to those in institutional advancement. It includes numerous checklists and samples, along with suggested steps, do's and don't's, and other advice. Ready reference sections provide information on postal and copyright regulations, direct-mail organizations, and directories of principal businesses.

230 Hopkins, Bruce R. *Charity Under Seige: Government Regulation of Fund Raising.* New York: Wiley, 1981. 274 pages.

This work analyzes legal and constitutional issues concerning state and federal regulations of fund-raising activities. More than half is devoted to a state-by-state review and comparative summary of the existing laws and regulations governing charitable fund raising. Among the IRS regulations examined are unrelated-income rules, reporting requirements, lobbying restrictions, charity classifications, and record-retention requirements for educational institutions. A useful set of appendixes includes a chart of state laws, bibliographies, and basic standards of fund raising and philanthropy.

231 Hopkins, Bruce R. *Charitable Giving and Tax Exempt Organizations: The Impact of the 1981 Tax Act.* New York: Wiley, 1982. 166 pages.

This book provides a detailed analysis of the 1981 tax act and how it affects charitable giving and tax-exempt organizations. It examines the new rules regarding charitable giving and tax-exempt organizations and discusses some of their adverse effects on charitable giving. Appendixes contain pertinent provisions of the Economic Recovery Tax Act of 1981 and estimated revenue effects.

232 Hunt, Susan (ed.). *New Sources of Revenue: An Ideabook.* Washington, D.C.: Council for Advancement and Support of Education, 1984. 64 pages.

This publication examines new approaches to generating revenue and noncash resources, details an analytical process that can help colleges and universities identify new resources, and addresses legal and tax considerations. It provides case studies of successful new enterprises at educational institutions around the country. Examples of revenue-producing activities are grouped into nine categories: investment and financial strategies; land sale, lease, or sale-leaseback; rental of facilities and space; profit-making ventures; joint ventures with business and industry; reduction of expenditures; nonfinancial resources; innovative ways to pay for a college education; and tuition-assistance programs.

233 Hunter, T. Willard. *The Tax Climate for Philanthropy.* Washington, D.C.: American College Public Relations Association, 1968. 207 pages.

This book presents the results of a study exploring the issues concerning tax deductability for philanthropical contributions and speculates on the effect that the abolition of tax deductability would have on such contributions. It includes an examination of tax laws and philosophical issues and a review of proposals and their prospects, along with Hunter's recommendations.

234 Huntsinger, Jerry. *Fund-Raising Letters: A Comprehensive Study Guide to Raising Money by Direct Response Marketing.* Richmond, Va.: Emerson, 1984. 400 pages.

This comprehensive manual on direct-response marketing explains how to write fund-raising letters, how to create a fund-raising package, how to apply computers to direct-response marketing, and how to manage fund-raising activities. It includes a special section on the use of multimedia fund raising and provides advice on developing a marketing strategy.

235 Lant, Jeffrey L. *Development Today: A Guide for Non-Profit Organizations.* Hartsdale, N.Y.: Public Service Materials Center, 1984. 200 pages.

This practical tool provides nonprofit organizations with useful and detailed information on fund raising from individuals, corporations, and foundations. It covers such topics as organizing the fund-raising function, producing fund-raising documents, who should be involved and what they should do, and how to organize staff and volunteer services. It provides advice on capital-fund drives, special events, direct mail, and applying for federal grants, with over seventy pages of sample materials.

236 Lautman, Kay Partney, and Goldstein, Henry. *Dear Friend: Mastering the Art of Direct Mail Fund Raising.* Washington, D.C.: Taft Corporation, 1983. 300 pages.

This step-by-step guide to all aspects of direct-mail fund raising explores the many possibilities of direct-mail campaigns and discusses how to raise money for a wide range of causes at the lowest possible price.

237 Lord, James Gregory. *Philanthropy and Marketing: New Strategies for Fund Raising.* Cleveland, Ohio: Third Sector Press, 1981. 270 pages.

Drawing on years of marketing and fund-raising experience, the author combines both areas to construct a new and practical framework from which to operate. This book describes how to build a fund-raising case into an effective marketing tool and how to include donors in the planning. It provides sample questionnaires for conducting donor research, a checklist of materials for donors and volunteers, and fourteen questions to answer before developing a fund-raising case. It also contains a psychological profile of the big donor.

★**238** Marquis Academic Media. *Annual Register of Grant Support: A Directory of Funding Sources, 1984–85.* (18th ed.) Chicago: Marquis Professional Publications, 1985. 899 pages.

Now in its eighteenth edition, this register is an authoritative standard reference of sources of grant support. The 1984–85 edition includes details of grant-support programs of government agencies, public and private foundations, corporations, community trusts, unions, educational and professional associations, and special-interest organizations. Each program description contains details of the type, purpose, and duration of the grant, the amount of funding available for each award, eligibility requirements, application instructions and deadlines, and personnel of the funding organization, as well as its address, founding date, telephone number, and areas of interest. Four indexes—subject, organization and program, geographical, and personnel—facilitate the potential applicant's search. There are 2,873 entries in this edition.

★**239** Marts, Arnaud C. *The Generosity of Americans: Its Source, Its Achievements.* Englewood Cliffs, N.J.: Prentice-Hall, 1966. 240 pages.

This classic work traces the private generosity for public good as a distinctive and dynamic force in Western civilization. It describes how billions of dollars from private sources have helped to create and assist thousands of private and public service, cultural, and educational organizations and institutions.

240 Panas, Jerold. *Mega Gifts: Who Gives Them, Who Gets Them.* Washington, D.C.: Taft Corporation, 1984. 224 pages.

In this book, twenty-two prominent donors give the inside story on why they gave a million dollars or more to a variety of institutions. The book offers help in understanding the motivation behind large gifts and discusses sixty-five guidelines for soliciting gifts from major donors. The insights offered, based on extensive interviewing by the author, are of practical value to all those involved in soliciting gifts from major donors.

241 Pendleton, Neil. *Fund Raising: A Guide for Non-Profit Organizations.* Englewood Cliffs, N.J.: Prentice-Hall, 1981. 207 pages.

This manual, geared toward salaried development officers, trustees, administrators, and volunteers, outlines the necessary steps to conducting successful fund-raising efforts for charitable, educational, and religious institutions or nonprofit organizations.

242 Pickett, William L. "What Determines Fund-Raising Effectiveness?" *CASE Currents,* 1984, *10,* 45–48.

The key question raised by Pickett in this study is "Why do some colleges raise more money than others?" He measured four variables: available resources; number of families with annual incomes of more than $50,000 in the standard metropolitan statistical area (SMSA) nearest the college; total number of grants made by major foundations located in the college's home state; and value added by manufacture in the SMSA nearest the college. This article, based on current research, should be read by all fund-raising professionals.

243 Pickett, William L. (ed.). "Part Three: Educational Fund-Raising." In A. Westley Rowland (gen. ed.), *Handbook of Institutional Advancement: A Practical Guide to College and University Relations, Fund Raising, Alumni Relations, Government Relations, Publications, and Executive Management for Continued Advancement.* (2nd ed.) San Francisco: Jossey-Bass, 1986. 130 pages.

This part of the *Handbook* offers detailed advice on all types of fund raising, presenting the best and most current thinking on the important components of educational fund raising. The opening chapter addresses two major issues that have direct impact on the success of individual fund-raising efforts: fund-raising effectiveness and why people make gifts. Succeeding chapters offer in-depth discussion of organizing and staffing the development office, the annual giving program, working with corporations and foundations, capital campaigns, planned giving (sometimes called deferred giving or estate planning), ways to secure major gifts, the importance and methods of research, records, and reports, and how to use professional counsel. (For a description of the *Handbook* in its entirety, see entry number 54.)

244 Pifer, Alan. *Philanthropy in an Age of Transition: The Essays of Alan Pifer*. New York: Foundation Center, 1984. 270 pages.

In these essays, collected from the annual reports of the Carnegie Corporation during the period 1966 to 1982, Alan Pifer analyzes philanthropy and other related issues of concern, including the responsibilities of higher education, charitable deductions, women in the work force, the financial straits of the nonprofit sector, the changing age composition of the American population, bilingual education, the progress of blacks, and more.

★**245** Pray, Francis C. (ed.). *Handbook for Educational Fund Raising: A Guide to Successful Principles and Practices for Colleges, Universities, and Schools*. San Francisco: Jossey-Bass, 1981. 442 pages.

Drawing on the advice of more than seventy development professionals, this handbook covers the full scope of educational fund raising. It is organized into twelve major sections, including annual giving, capital campaigns and major gifts, organizing and motivating volunteers, planning, strengthening relations with college constituencies, and increasing staff effectiveness. This valuable source for all educational fund raisers provides practical guidelines and checklists, makes specific recommendations, and gives examples of successful programs at a variety of institutions.

246 Public Management Institute. *Direct Mail Fund Raising.* San Francisco: Public Management Institute, 1980. 467 pages.

This simple, step-by-step approach to direct-mail fund raising covers the finding of new donors, mailing lists, creating effective mailing pieces, and cutting postage and printing costs. The manual's planning forms, checklists, and extensive samples demonstrate how to avoid costly mistakes, set up a revolving fund to minimize investment and maximize contributions, and start your own direct-mail program.

247 Reilley, Timothy A. *Raising Money Through an Institutionally Related Foundation.* Washington, D.C.: Council for Advancement and Support of Education, 1985. 83 pages.

This book provides an in-depth look at the foundations that serve nonprofit institutions, mainly universities but also two-year colleges and medical institutions. Various chapters explore how foundations related to nonprofit organizations are organized and controlled, how they exercise their functions, and how they operate as separate institutions. The work highlights the salient features of a foundation: its basic policies, its general patterns of control and operations, and how it achieves its objectives. This publication should prove invaluable both to institutions seeking to establish foundations and to existing foundations looking for new ideas and techniques for improving their operations.

248 Richards, Audrey (ed.). *The Complete Grants Sourcebook for Higher Education.* Washington, D.C.: Public Management Institute for the American Council on Education, 1980. 605 pages.

The first part of this book provides a step-by-step system for successful grant seeking, from organization preparation to proposal writing and follow-up. Part 2 contains more than 500 detailed entries for federal, foundation, and other programs of support. The book includes specific information on the funding resource's area of interest, financial data, eligibility requirements, application information, policy, and sample grants.

249 Schneiter, Paul H. *The Art of Asking: Handbook for Successful Fund Raising.* Ambler, Pa.: Fund-Raising Institute, 1978. 198 pages.

This basic and practical book on the full spectrum of fund-raising activities covers annual giving, capital campaigns, deferred giving, corporate and foundation solicitation, volunteers, and public relations. It elaborates on the various forms of soliciting in person, by proposal, by mail, with individuals, and with foundations and details how to prepare for and follow up on the requests.

250 Schneiter, Paul H., and Nelson, Donald T. *The Thirteen Most Common Fund-Raising Mistakes and How to Avoid Them.* Washington, D.C.: Taft Corporation, 1982. 90 pages.

This work addresses fund raising with a broad perspective and a sense of humor. Focusing on thirteen key fund-raising mistakes, the authors utilize colorful narratives and cartoons to capsulize the various facts and point out examples of fortunes and successes.

★251 Seymour, Harold J. *Design for Fund Raising.* New York: McGraw-Hill, 1966. 210 pages.

This book, a classic in the profession, offers a wealth of practical and theoretical guidance on the personal aspects of fund raising. It examines people's motivations and describes the importance of taking time to cultivate a prospective donor's interest. One-fourth of the book is devoted to the capital campaign, discussing the crucial fund-raising tripod of annual giving, capital campaigns, and bequest programs. Also covered are such aspects of fund raising as public relations, working with consultants, and writing.

252 Sharpe, Robert F. *Before You Give Another Dime.* Nashville, Tenn.: Nelson, 1979. 189 pages.

This book, written for individuals who are interested in making donations to charitable organizations, offers advice in planning gifts, choosing what to give, how much, and when, and how to give. It covers the giving of cash, stocks and bonds, real estate, and personal possessions, as well as giving through revocable living trusts, retirement plans, and wills, suggests ways potential donors can increase the effectiveness of their gifts, and discusses relevant tax laws.

253 Sheppard, William E. *Fund-Raising Letter Collection.* Ambler, Pa.: Fund-Raising Institute, 1977. 150 pages.

A combination album and textbook, this work illustrates a wide assortment of successful fund-raising letters that can be adapted to a variety of needs. Types of letters included are thank-yous, class-agent letters, membership-solicitation letters, hard-sell letters, novelty letters, and others. Editorial comments explain the whys and hows of each letter's effectiveness. The book also includes chapters on how to write a fund-raising letter, the ideal direct-mail package, money-making ways to open and close a letter, and computer-generated mailings.

254 Taft Corporation. *America's Wealthiest People: Their Philanthropic and Nonprofit Affiliations.* Washington, D.C.: Taft Corporation, 1984. 80 pages.

This publication presents pertinent biographical data on more than 500 of America's wealthiest individuals, with estimated net wealth of up to $2.2 billion. Data include employment, office and home address, date and state of birth, educational background, club memberships, sources and estimates of wealth, and other valuable details, with general information on the philanthropical involvement of these individuals, both their individual gifts and their affiliations with foundations and other nonprofit organizations.

255 Taft Corporation. *People in Philanthropy.* Washington, D.C.: Taft Corporation, 1985. 400 pages.

This authoritative volume comprises bibliographical profiles on 8,000 of the wealthiest individuals, major donors, foundation trustees, and corporate philanthropical officers. Key indexes include place of birth, alma mater, and philanthropical connections to help trustees, directors, and others analyze information from the $60 billion treasury of private giving in America. The book makes the case that all institutions have people-related connections that can enhance leverage in the philanthropical power structure.

★**256** White, Virginia P. *Grants: How to Find Out About Them and What to Do Next.* New York: Plenum, 1976. 354 pages.

This practical guide to grantsmanship covers everything you need to know before writing your first proposal. It includes information on what a grant is, sources of information, types of grants available, and the differences among government, foundation, and industry grants. It details the steps to take before you apply and how to write a proposal, discusses the criteria used by agencies in making awards, and provides examples of applications, and letters.

257 White, Virginia P. (ed.). *Grant Proposals That Succeeded.* New York: Plenum, 1983. 248 pages.

In this compendium of grant-winning proposals from universities, colleges, research organizations, human service agencies, and cultural groups, White gives a point-by-point explanation of the processes that went into securing the grant (initial research, selection of prospective agency, personal meetings, and pregrant negotiations) as well as critiques on what made the proposal strong.

258 Winship, Addison L. (ed.). *The Quest for Major Gifts* Washington, D.C.: Council for Advancement and Support of Education, 1984. 56 pages.

This publication reports the results of a survey conducted with sixty-eight CASE member institutions. It discusses how major gifts are being cultivated and solicited and covers the general definition of major gifts, staff requirements, solicitation procedures, and requirements for endowed professorships as well as other specific endowments.

259 Worth, Michael J. *Public College and University Development*. Washington, D.C.: Council for Advancement and Support of Education, 1985. 164 pages.

This volume is addressed to development officers in the public sector to help them better understand the circumstances and opportunities facing their institutions. The focus in this book is not on techniques or "how to do it"; rather, the purpose is to provide a discussion of the ways in which fund raising in the public sector differs from that in the private sector and how such differences affect the strategies that must be pursued.

Annual Giving

260 Balthaser, William F. *Call for Help: How to Raise Philanthropic Funds with Phonathons*. Ambler, Pa.: Fund-Raising Institute, 1984. 158 pages.

This easy-to-read and thorough guide to the whole "phonathon" process presents step-by-step instructions on how to plan, organize, and conduct a phonathon. It includes numerous sample letters, scripts, and forms and covers such basic information as whom to call and how to find them, how to design the message, when to call (best months, days, and hours), how to arrange for the calling site and supplies, and an estimate of the costs and benefits of phonathons.

261 Carter, Virginia L. (ed.). *Annual Fund Ideas*. Washington, D.C.: Council for Advancement and Support of Education, 1979. 48 pages.

This is a spiral-bound collection featuring forty of the best *CASE Currents* articles on how to plan, organize, and carry out a successful annual fund. It includes material on class agents, challenge gifts, matching gifts, parent funds, reunion gifts, and raising funds by mail.

262 Council for Advancement and Support of Education. "Gift Clubs." *CASE Currents,* 1980, *6* (10), 7–29.

In this special insert of *CASE Currents,* there are seven articles that discuss various aspects of gift clubs, ranging from the purposes they can serve and how to select membership criteria to descriptions of how they are operating at different institutions. In between, there is plenty of advice on how to enroll and entertain members, set goals, use volunteers, and say "thank you" properly.

263 Council for Advancement and Support of Education. "The Annual Fund." *CASE Currents,* 1982, *8* (entire issue 9).

This special issue of *CASE Currents* is devoted entirely to components of a successful annual-giving program. The ten articles included cover planning and managing the annual fund and explain techniques such as personal solicitation, phonathons, direct mail, class agents, reunion giving, and senior class giving.

264 Council for Advancement and Support of Education. "Parents Programs." *CASE Currents,* 1985, *11* (entire issue 6).

This special issue of *CASE Currents* discusses various aspects of parents' programs, including coverage of Princeton University's parents' fund, new ways to involve parents, and the planning of parents' sessions during student orientation. This is a valuable group of articles for those who are interested in starting a parents' program.

265 Cover, Nelson (ed.). *A Guide to Successful Phonathons.* (Rev. ed.) Washington, D.C.: Council for Advancement and Support of Education, 1984. 95 pages.

This publication presents everything you need to know about how to raise money through phonathons. The authors outline how to set up a timetable, secure facilities, recruit and train volunteers, and follow through with thank-you letters, with down-to-earth advice on when to call, whether to serve food and drink, and how to develop an "upbeat" attitude that leads to more calls and bigger gifts. The extensive appendix contains sample letters, forms, and instructions for workers.

266 Sheppard, William E. *Annual Giving Idea Book*. Ambler, Pa.: Fund-Raising Institute, 1977. 415 pages.

In this presentation of practical ideas for immediate and profitable use in raising annual gifts, the author presents ten steps for taking control of an annual-giving program or starting one from scratch. Among the topics he discusses are how to find first-time givers, how to get repeat gifts, the basics of writing annual-giving letters, and how to conduct an annual-giving phonathon. Sheppard includes samples of materials from several colleges and universities.

267 Sweeney, Robert D. (ed.). *Raising Money Through Gift Clubs: A Survey of Techniques at 42 Institutions*. Washington, D.C.: Council for Advancement and Support of Education, 1982. 71 pages.

This work offers an inside look at how colleges, universities, and independent schools use gift clubs to motivate donors to make substantial gifts. It covers starting a club program, requirements for membership, methods for enlisting members, suggested programs and activities, perquisites offered to members, upgrading gifts, and estimating program costs.

★268 Welch, Patrice A. (ed.). *Increasing Annual Giving*. New Directions for Institutional Advancement, no. 7. San Francisco: Jossey-Bass, 1980. 112 pages.

This sourcebook discusses the role of the annual fund in the total development program and reports on recent trends in annual giving. It describes techniques for increasing the effectiveness of annual fund programs in such areas as goal setting, staffing, recruiting and training volunteers, targeting direct mail, and using telethons.

269 Williams, M. Jane. *The FRI Annual Giving Book.* Ambler, Pa.: Fund-Raising Institute, 1981. 415 pages.

This book focuses on annual giving as the cornerstone upon which all other fund-raising programs are built and the place where all good development programs begin. It provides details on 150 annual campaigns and successful programs and gives straightforward advice on how to prepare and launch an annual giving program, looking specifically at challenge programs, phonathons, and minimum-gift clubs. Many of the examples are drawn from colleges and universities, including such institutions as Harvard, Yale, Johns Hopkins, and others.

Foundation Grants

★**270** Council for Advancement and Support of Education. "Cultivating Foundations." *CASE Currents,* 1984, *10* (entire issue 7).

This issue of *CASE Currents,* devoted to articles on foundation support, includes advice from a foundation president, explains how to apply for and win grants from both large and small foundations, and describes ways in which the telephone can be useful in the cultivation process. It also includes a bibliography of foundation research resources.

271 Dermer, Joseph. *The New How to Raise Funds From Foundations.* (3rd ed.) Hartsdale, N.Y.: Public Service Materials Center, 1981. 95 pages.

This practical manual covers every aspect of foundation fund raising, from writing proposals to getting appointments. A new method of getting appointments with foundation officials is spelled out in this new edition.

272 Dermer, Joseph (ed.). *Where America's Large Foundations Make Their Grants: 1983-84 Edition.* Hartsdale, N.Y.: Public Service Materials Center, 1984. 256 pages.

This book offers a full range of information on the specifics of grant making by over 650 of the largest foundations in America, including information on types of grants awarded, purpose, previous grantees, application processes, and range of awards. It also includes information on current changes within foundations and tips on how to approach them.

273 Foundation Center. *Foundation Fundamentals.* (3rd ed.) New York: Foundation Center, 1981. 148 pages.

This basic and straightforward guide to applying for funds from foundations provides the reader with a step-by-step guide through the funding-research process and contains illustrations, worksheets, and checklists to help start the search for funding. Comprehensive bibliographies and detailed research examples are also provided. This work is most useful for newcomers.

274 Foundation Center. *Comsearch Printouts: Broad Topics.* New York: Foundation Center, 1984. Variable pages.

This publication presents computer-produced listings of foundation grants in the broad topic areas of art; cultural programs; business and employment; children and youth; higher education; hospitals and health care; museums; science programs; social science programs; women and girls; international and foreign programs; minorities; religion and religious education; public health; public policy and political science; recreation; community and urban development; and elementary and secondary education. Each topic guidebook lists foundations that grant awards in the topic area, with address and phone number, listing of awards, special restrictions, and application procedure. Each topic book is indexed by recipient name, recipient state, and key words.

275 Foundation Center. *Comsearch Printouts: Geographic.* New York: Foundation Center, 1984. Variable pages.

This publication lists actual grants made to organizations in Washington, D.C., and in eleven states (including California, Massachusetts, New York, Ohio, Pennsylvania, Texas, and Michigan). It covers primarily the Northeast, Southeast, Northwest, and Rocky Mountains regions.

276 Foundation Center. *Comsearch Printouts: Special Topics.* New York: Foundation Center, 1984. Variable pages.

This publication consists of computer printouts of the 1,000 largest U.S. foundations by asset size, the 1,000 largest U.S. foundations by annual grants total, and 1,400 operating foundations that administer their own projects or programs.

277 Foundation Center. *Comsearch Printouts: Subjects.* New York: Foundation Center, 1984. Variable pages.

These sixty-two computer-produced subject guides to foundation grants list actual grants made, arranged alphabetically by state, by foundation name, and by recipient. Among the subjects included are capital support for higher education, endowments for higher education, matching and challenge grants, educational research, and conferences and seminars.

278 Foundation Center. *Source Book Profiles.* New York: Foundation Center, 1984. Variable pages.

This quarterly publication covers the 1,000 largest foundations in a two-year publishing cycle, with 500 foundations analyzed each quarter. Each profile is four to six pages long and includes address and phone number, names of officers and staff members, giving limitations, financial data, background information, publications, application guidelines, sample grants, and grants analysis. The listings are indexed by subject, type of support, foundation name, location, and focus of giving.

★**279** Foundation Center. *The Foundation Directory*. (10th ed.) New York: Foundation Center, 1985. 761 pages.

The tenth edition of this yearly directory provides fund raisers with information on 4,400 private foundations that have more than $63 billion in assets and award $4.1 billion in grants annually. It is indexed by name, city and state, donor, trustees and administrators, and field of interest. Listings include donor, purpose and activities, financial data, and application procedures. The work also includes a glossary, an annotated bibliography of Foundation Center publications and services, an analysis of foundation funding trends, and a general introduction to fund raising from foundations.

280 Foundation Center. *Foundation Directory Supplement*. (10th ed.) New York: Foundation Center, 1985. 428 pages.

This supplement to the tenth edition of the *Foundation Directory* (see entry number 279) updates entries for 2,000 of the 4,400 foundations listed.

281 Freeman, David F. *The Handbook of Private Foundations*. Cabin John, Md., and Washington, D.C.: Seven Locks Press for the Council on Foundations, 1981. 435 pages.

This book provides a comprehensive, practical guide to the environment in which foundations must function and the rules and regulations by which they must operate. It also offers an inside look at the grant-making process, the influences that shape policies and define program interests, and the internal structures and practices that enhance the overall operations of foundations.

282 Public Service Materials Center. *The 1983-84 Survey of Grant Making Foundations*. Hartsdale, N.Y.: Public Service Materials Center, 1984. 94 pages.

This work contains vital information on nearly 1,000 foundations, each having assets of over $1 million or awarding grants of more than $100,000. Information includes best time of year to approach the foundation; whether the foundation makes appointments and who should be contacted; whether it makes operating, building, or renovation grants and what geographical restrictions are placed on these; and which foundations plan to increase grant giving.

283 Ross, J. David (ed.). *Understanding and Increasing Foundation Support.* New Directions for Institutional Advancement, no. 11. San Francisco: Jossey-Bass, 1981. 94 pages.

In addition to analyzing key developments in foundation funding, such as the impact of recent tax legislation, this guide explains how to seek foundation support. It provides suggestions on researching foundations, grant writing, and solicitations and addresses the development of new approaches for the 1980s.

★**284** Taft Corporation. *The Taft Foundation Reporter.* New York: Taft Corporation, 1984. 700 pages.

This directory covers more than 500 of the largest national and regional private foundations. Entries for each foundation list type of foundation, types of grants, grant distribution, contact person, with address and phone number, fiscal information, background information on areas of interest, analyses of previous grants, and biographical sketches of officers and directors. The work is indexed by field of interest, state, foundation managers, and trustees by state of birth and alma mater. This is the only directory that provides biographical data on foundation officers and directors.

285 Williams, M. Jane (ed.). *Foundations Handbook.* (3rd ed.) Ambler, Pa.: Fund-Raising Institute, 1975. 130 pages.

This collection of practical instructions, supplemented with easily adaptable examples, looks at who, what, and where the foundations are and explains how to research and seek foundation support. Foundation officials answer the four most common questions regarding grant seeking: how to approach foundations, how to make presentations, what type of presentations are best, and how long it takes for foundations to respond. Sample proposals, letters of intent, and successful grant applications from a variety of educational and noneducational organizations are included.

286 Williams, M. Jane. *Foundation Primer*. Ambler, Pa.: Fund-Raising Institute, 1980. 152 pages.

This book offers a step-by-step organization plan, as well as detailed techniques for proposal writing, personal solicitation, and follow-up. All chapters include examples of letters, forms, and proposals. The beginning chapters, covering the nature and workings of foundations, are particularly helpful to the newcomer. The book also discusses the principles of starting and staffing a successful foundation-solicitation program and includes a discussion of the Fund-Raising Institute's "foundation solicitation formula," which describes how to find the right foundation, create sellable projects, and develop a game plan for each prospect, as well as other important details.

Corporate Grants

287 Brodsky, Jean (ed.). *Taft Corporate Foundation Directory*. Washington, D.C.: Taft Corporation, 1977. 373 pages.

This volume contains detailed individual profiles on 276 company-sponsored foundations, representing corporations with facilities in all fifty states, the District of Columbia, and numerous foreign countries. Profiles are organized to provide complete information on the company itself and the areas of funding interest for each one. Grant information for each company-sponsored foundation includes range and average size of grant and sample of previous grant awards.

288 Conrad, Daniel Lynn. *How to Get Corporate Grants*. San Francisco: Public Management Institute, 1984. 351 pages.

Using a systematic approach, this manual shows how to identify those corporations that are most likely to support your organization, how to reach corporate decision makers, how to effectively use board members, volunteers, and others, and how to present your case so that it meets your needs and those of the corporation's. It contains a number of checklists, forms, and worksheets.

★**289** Council for Advancement and Support of Education. "Corporate Support." *CASE Currents*, 1981, 7 (entire issue 10).

This special issue of *CASE Currents* covers all aspects of corporate support: how to interest and involve corporations; how small colleges, women's colleges, and community colleges gain corporate support; how to use matching-gift programs; and what to do after you get corporate support. Other articles describe a day in the life of a corporate contributions officer and explore the question: Will corporations take up the slack left by Reaganomics?

★**290** Council for Advancement and Support of Education. *Guidelines for the Administration of Matching Gift Programs.* Report of the joint task force on matching gifts of the Council for Advancement and Support of Education, the National Council of University Business Officers, and the Council for Financial Aid to Education. Washington, D.C.: Council for Advancement and Support of Education, 1983. 15 pages.

This booklet presents recommendations for administering matching-gift programs so that growth continues while flexibility is maintained. It addresses specific ways that matching-gift administrators can build upon sound procedures, outlines general program controls, and discusses the responsibilities of the sponsoring company, the donors, and the recipient institutions. The work includes examples of model matching-gift programs.

291 Council for Advancement and Support of Education. *Double Your Dollar 1984–1985*. Washington, D.C.: Council for Advancement and Support of Education, 1984. 174 pages.

This publication, updated annually, lists all companies that currently match employee gifts in the areas of higher education, secondary and elementary schools, nonprofit cultural organizations, public television and radio, and nonprofit hospitals and health and social service organizations. Leaflets coded for special program details are designed as direct-mail pieces for mailing to alumni and potential donors.

292 Council for Advancement and Support of Education. *Profiles: Educational Institutions*. Washington, D.C.: Council for Advancement and Support of Education, 1985. 1,200 pages.

This guidebook brings together all the data a company needs to know when it is considering an institution for matching gifts. More than 4,000 institutions are listed, including universities, colleges, secondary and elementary schools, and special education institutions. The data collected for each institution are presented in the areas of institutional profile, institutional contacts, institution foundation, 1982–83 matching-gift program, matching-gift auditing history, and donor gift recognition.

★293 Council for Financial Aid to Education. *CFAE Corporate Handbook*. New York: Council for Financial Aid to Education, 1984. 232 pages.

This book contains a descriptive sampling of 203 leading corporations that have established programs of support to education, either through foundations or otherwise. Each corporate educational support program is described in a profile outlining amount of gifts to education in the previous year, general purposes of support, and types of support granted. Breakdowns of giving include amounts given for unrestricted operating grants, departmental and research grants, matching gifts, and indirect grants through other organizations.

294 Dermer, Joseph, and Wertheimer, Stephen (ed.). *The Complete Guide to Corporate Fund Raising.* Hartsdale, N.Y.: Public Service Materials Center, 1982. 112 pages.

This manual explains how to write a corporate proposal, enlist and work with corporate volunteers, get appointments with corporate officials, do research on corporations, avoid the five most common mistakes that grant seekers make, and more. It offers many examples to illustrate corporate fund raising from the vantage points of a university, a hospital, a cultural institution, and others.

295 Foundation Center. *Corporate Foundation Profiles.* (3rd ed.) New York: Foundation Center, 1983. 550 pages.

In this detailed analysis of 230 of the largest company-sponsored foundations in the United States, three- to six-page entries include information on location, board and officer affiliations, types of support offered, financial summaries, and more. Financial summaries are also provided for an additional 400 corporate foundations that give more than $100,000 annually and have over $1 million in assets.

★296 Hall, Elizabeth S. (ed.). *Matching Gifts Details 1984.* Washington, D.C.: Council for Advancement and Support of Education, 1984. 174 pages.

This comprehensive guide lists program details of 916 companies currently offering matching employee gifts to colleges, universities, and independent schools. Individual company entries, which expand on information in *Double Your Dollar* leaflets (see entry number 291), provide all the information necessary for matching-gift program administration. Details on companies include eligibility requirements, requirements of beneficiary institution, minimum and maximum awards, types of awards, contacts, and special terms and conditions.

297 Hickey, James W. (ed.). *Taft Trustees of Wealth: A Biographical Directory of Private Foundation and Corporate Foundation Officers.* (5th ed.) Washington, D.C.: Taft Corporation, 1979. 565 pages.

This directory lists biographical data for 7,600 trustees and officers representing 4,500 family, general-purpose, corporate, community, and operating foundations. Biographical material includes educational background, club membership, corporate and non-profit affiliations, place of residence, and past and present employment. Indexes cross reference individuals by foundations and by state. This is a useful tool for systematic prospect research and the targeting of appropriate individuals to cultivate and solicit as potential donors.

298 Hillman, Howard. *The Art of Winning Corporate Grants.* New York: Vanguard Press, 1980. 180 pages.

This practical guide to successfully approaching corporations is based on Hillman's assumption that "virtually all donations are made in the self-interest of the corporation." Topics include why and how corporations give and to whom, how to research corporation prospects, how to approach corporations, how to put together a proposal that corporations will fund, and how to follow through. The guide contains an idea-packed section filled with many examples.

299 Podesta, Aldo C. *Raising Funds from America's 2,000,000 Overlooked Corporations.* Hartsdale, N.Y.: Public Service Materials Center, 1984. 118 pages.

This book provides details on how to locate, approach, and win grants from what are referred to as the "hidden corporations" (local and/or low-profile corporations). It tells how to research corporations and select the best ones, how to arrange meetings with officials, how to enlist corporate leaders as volunteers, and it offers ten winning tips on preparing a proposal.

300 Public Management Institute. *Corporate 500: The Directory of Corporate Philanthropy.* (4th ed.) San Francisco: Public Management Institute, 1985. 942 pages.

This directory provides information on 540 corporations that give directly or through associated foundations. The information, which has been verified by the corporations, includes business profile, activities currently supported, eligibility requirements, funds available, range of awards by type and average amount, application process, and sample grants. Indexes are arranged by twelve categories, including funding areas, state, region, corporate headquarters, officers and trustees, and eligible activities.

301 Public Service Materials Center. *The Corporate Fund Raising Directory—1985-86 Edition.* Hartsdale, N.Y.: Public Service Materials Center, 1984. 400 pages.

This reference book provides comprehensive information on 625 of America's foremost corporations. Each entry includes name, address, and telephone number, contact person, application procedure, geographical preference, and past award information, such as total number of grants, range of grants, names of previous grantees, and areas of giving. Grant seekers are offered guidance and advice on the best time to approach each corporation, which corporations expect to increase their giving, which will issue guidelines, and which will contribute executives and materials as well as dollars. The directory is indexed by geographical location, subject, and corporate name.

302 Public Service Materials Center. *Grant Making Corporations That Publish Guidelines.* Hartsdale, N.Y.: Public Service Materials Center, 1984. 45 pages.

This work lists the names, addresses, and telephone numbers of 227 grant-making corporations that publish guidelines for grant seekers and will mail them upon request. This tool helps save many hours of research and assures access to the most current information.

303 Sinclair, James P. *How to Write Successful Corporate Appeals—with Full Examples.* Hartsdale, N.Y.: Public Service Materials Center, 1982. 110 pages.

This book explains how to make effective appeals to corporations, beginning with a review of a variety of grant-seeking situations and then offering useful insights and tips that are applicable to these situations. It provides instructions on how to write letters that get appointments, help sell proposals, win grants, and propose new buildings and renovations, as well as covering special project proposals, renewal letters, cultivation letters, and thank-you letters. Multiple examples include a variety of sample proposals, cover letters, and budgets.

304 Taft Corporation. *Corporate Giving Yellow Pages.* New York: Taft Corporation, 1984. 88 pages.

This publication lists philanthropical contact persons at 1,100 of America's leading publicly and privately owned corporations that currently operate direct-giving programs or corporate foundations. It is indexed by state of corporate headquarters and type of business.

★**305** Taft Corporation. *The Taft Corporate Giving Directory.* Taft Corporation, 1985. 750 pages.

This directory provides detailed coverage of corporate giving. More than 530 of the largest corporate giving programs are reviewed, including corporate foundations as well as direct-giving programs. Entries include biographical data on corporate officials and trustees, types of grants given typical recipients, giving priorities, and budget. Eight indexes include corporate officers by state of birth and alma mater, operating locations, type of grant, type of recipient, corporate headquarters, and sponsoring company.

Capital Campaigns

306 Colodren, Sharon. *The Constant Quest: Raising Billions Through Capital Campaigns.* Washington, D.C.: American Council on Education, 1982. 118 pages.

This book reports on the findings of a survey on capital campaigns at colleges and universities between 1974 and 1984 conducted by the Council for Financial Aid to Education and the American Council for Education. The report examines the goals of capital campaigns, who its contributors are, the purposes for which funds are used, and how capital campaigns are conducted. Among its conclusions are that colleges are quite successful in achieving their campaign goals, that individuals provide 89 percent of all funds, and that nearly one-half of the funds are used for endowment funding.

★**307** Council for Advancement and Support of Education. "The Capital Campaign." *CASE Currents,* 1979, *5* (entire issue 3).

This special issue of *CASE Currents* features articles that offer practical advice on running a capital campaign. Techniques covered include how to involve the president and volunteers, prepare a precampaign survey, identify and nurture key prospects, enlist and train effective campaign leaders, and design public relations materials. The articles discuss the changing forms of the capital campaign and how the annual-giving, deferred-giving, and capital campaigns can work together successfully.

308 Council for Advancement and Support of Education. *PR Support in the Capital Campaign.* Washington, D.C.: Council for Advancement and Support of Education, 1983. 6 pages.

This publication explains why the capital campaign needs effective public relations, how to create a public relations plan to boost a major campaign, and how to involve alumni who have media connections.

309 Council for Advancement and Support of Education. "Terms of Endowment." *CASE Currents,* 1985, *11* (entire issue 5).

This special edition of *CASE Currents* focusing on endowments includes eight articles that discuss an endowment strategy, a recipe for endowment growth, the National Council of University Business Officers' study (which answers donor questions), ten steps to increase endowment, how to write a case statement, and how to publish a campaign newsletter.

310 Public Management Institute. *Capital Campaign Resource Guide.* San Francisco: Public Management Institute, 1985. 1,200 pages.

This new five-part directory on capital campaigns provides profiles on 100 foundations and 150 corporations that contribute to capital campaigns, a directory of state laws regulating fund raising, over 160 pages of forms, checklists, and worksheets, a national directory of fund-raising consultants, and a list of over 1,500 nonprofit organizations that have recently conducted capital campaigns and will provide information and advice upon request. The "how-to" section maps out 130 detailed topics in an easy-to-understand format. The fifteen indexes also help make this a quick and easy directory to use.

311 Williams, M. Jane. *FRI Capital Ideas.* 2 vols. Ambler, Pa.: Fund-Raising Institute, 1979. 320 pages.

These handbooks provide the elements and techniques of a systematic approach to capital fund raising. Volume 1 offers a general treatment of capital campaigns, while volume 2 elaborates on successful capital campaigns in four institutions: a church, a hospital, a private college, and a public university. In addition, case histories are provided for five colleges and universities, five medical institutions, and five miscellaneous campaigns.

Deferred Giving

★**312** Carter, Virginia L., and Garigan, Catherine S. (eds.). *Planned Giving Ideas.* Washington, D.C.: Council for Advancement and Support of Education, 1979. 30 pages.

In this book, Carter and Garigan pull together material from two special issues of *CASE Currents* on planned giving. It includes articles on institutional commitment and policies and programs to encourage various types of gifts—bequests, unitrusts, annuity trusts, charitable income trusts (lead trusts), pooled-income funds, and gifts of land—as well as how to hire planned-giving officers.

★**313** Council for Advancement and Support of Education. "Planned Giving: Part I." *CASE Currents,* 1979, *5* (entire issue 10).

The nine articles in this special issue of *CASE Currents,* the first in a two-part series (see also entry number 314), provides a general overview of planned giving. Articles focus on such planned-giving programs as pooled-income trust funds, charitable trusts, deferred giving, gifts of land, and annuities. Also included are discussions of tax developments and their impact on planned giving and a look at what is involved in hiring a planned-giving officer, with advice on job descriptions, advertising, personnel selection, and training.

★**314** Council for Advancement and Support of Education. "Planned Giving: Part II." *CASE Currents,* 1979, *5* (entire issue 11).

In this special issue of *CASE Currents,* the series on planned giving concludes with a collection of how-to articles covering such tasks as cultivating donors, cooperating with their advisers, organizing volunteers, and working with the business office. (For a description of the first part of this series, see entry number 313.)

315 Council for Advancement and Support of Education. "Deferred Giving." *CASE Currents*, 1983, *9* (4), 24–36.

This three-article special insert in *CASE Currents* provides assistance in assessing whether an institution should set up a pooled-income fund. It provides an update on the tax savings available to donors and a discussion of the establishment of standard gift-reporting guidelines by CASE and the National Council of University Business Officers.

★**316** Dunseth, William. *An Introduction to Annuity, Charitable Remainder Trust, and Bequest Programs*. Washington, D.C.: Council for Advancement and Support of Education, 1982. 37 pages.

This handbook covers, in layperson's language, the various types of gifts and their tax advantages, how to start and market a program, how to work with the business office, and how to evaluate a program.

317 Fink, Norman S., and Metzler, Howard C. *The Costs and Benefits of Deferred Giving*. Hartsdale, N.Y.: Public Service Materials Center, 1981. 255 pages.

The authors of this book propose that deferred giving should ultimately account for one-third of an institution's income and detail how that goal can be reached. They examine the differences among various types of deferred giving, explain what type of charitable giving plan is best followed under which circumstances, and offer suggestions on how to market and promote a deferred-giving program for those who know the institution and those who do not. The book contains nearly 100 pages of examples, model forms, worksheets, and definitions.

318 Fund-Raising Institute. *Deferred-Giving Handbook*. Ambler, Pa.: Fund-Raising Institute, 1980. 123 pages.

This handbook describes how to begin a deferred-giving program and how to upgrade a current one. It explains the various deferred-giving methods (bequests, life-income plans, life insurance, pooled-income funds) and the basics of federal estate taxes, outlines such program basics as staffing, leadership, and management, provides quick pointers from other professionals in the fields, and includes many easy-to-adapt letters, booklets, forms, and surveys.

319 Holzman, Robert S. *Encyclopedia of Estate Planning.* (4th ed.) New York: Boardroom Books, 1980. 311 pages.

This comprehensive guide to estate planning is well written and easy to understand. Chapters discuss such topics as making a will, the different types of trusts available (short-term, spendthrift, generation-skipping, and charitable remainder), gifts, forms of ownership, sale and leaseback, insurance, bequests, using a corporation to transfer assets, annuities, and much more.

320 Kahn, Arnold D. *Family Security Through Estate Planning.* (2nd ed.) New York: McGraw-Hill, 1983. 203 pages.

Written by an attorney who specializes in estate planning, this book is of tremendous value to fund raisers who solicit planned gifts. The book is written for the layperson and discusses such topics as basic concepts of estate planning, how to develop an estate plan, and how to work effectively with an attorney. It includes numerous worksheets and tables and a glossary.

321 King, George. *Deferred Gifts: How to Get Them.* (4th ed.) Ambler, Pa.: Fund-Raising Institute, 1980. 200 pages.

This work describes the best proven ideas and techniques used by a wide variety of charities to acquire significant philanthropical income through deferred gifts, drawing on the experiences of more than fifty practitioners representing highly successful programs supporting many types of nonprofit organizations. The book emphasizes the practical promotional and managerial aspects of deferred giving, with more than 220 easy-to-adapt examples encompassing a variety of specific situations.

322 Public Management Institute. *How to Build a Big Endowment.* (Rev. ed.) San Francisco: Public Management Institute, 1984. 590 pages.

This manual provides detailed instructions on how to set up an endowment-development program, how to find the best prospects, how to convince donors to make large endowments, how to find and train staff and volunteers, and how to get gifts of stock, life insurance, real estate, and much more. It is especially helpful to those just starting endowments or seeking to increase their endowments through the use of a deferred-giving program. It includes hundreds of pages of forms, checklists, worksheets, and model promotions.

323 Resource Development. *Family Estate Planning Seminar.* Springfield, Mo.: Resource Development, 1983. 65 pages.

This book explains how charitable gifts can save on federal estate taxes. Topics include use of trusts, life insurance in estate planning, joint tenancy, and private annuities.

324 Sharpe, Robert F. *The Planned Giving Idea Book.* Nashville, Tenn.: Nelson, 1980. 285 pages.

This book, directed at college and university directors of development and others in the nonprofit sector, explains how to set up a planned-giving program and how to broaden and strengthen a present program to make it more effective. It suggests ways to encourage the use of revocable trusts, gift annuities, and pooled-income funds and to get an institution or organization included in donors' wills. It also explains how to attract life insurance and security gifts, how to set up trusts, how to raise foundation gifts, and how to apply the principles of memorial giving.

325 Vecchitto, Daniel W. (ed.). *An Introduction to Planned Giving: Fund Raising Through Bequests, Trusts, Gift Annuities and Life Insurance.* Nonprofit Technical Assistant Series, no. 2. Hartsdale, N.Y.: Public Service Materials Center, 1984. 179 pages.

In this manual, eight development experts offer useful information on how to start a planned-giving program, how to market it, and how to build relationships that will benefit both the institution and its prospective donors. It provides specific information on bequests, charitable remainder trusts, pooled-income funds, gift annuities, and life insurance and includes an up-to-date primer on federal tax laws that affect planned giving, a glossary of planned-giving terms, a directory of planned-giving resources, and a wide variety of sample forms.

5

Alumni Relations and Administration

The continued success of any college or university depends on its alumni. In a 1960 speech, Henry T. Heald, then president of the Ford Foundation, commented that "new generations of alumni provide the continuity that perpetuates a university. Its officers come and go, its faculty changes, its programs and buildings are replaced, but its alumni maintain a lifelong relationship with the university. They are keepers of the tradition, preferred stockholders of the enterprise, the mark of an accomplishment" (Rowland, 1977, p. 275).

Alumni relations is one of the oldest functions of colleges and universities. Alumni associations first began to be formed in the early 1800s; at that time, their activities were essentially social, centered on renewing old acquaintances and focusing on intercollegiate athletics, with little attention to the value alumni might have to their alma maters, or that the schools might have to their alumni. As fund-raising needs of institutions increased, however, they began turning for contributions to their alumni, who responded and continue to respond. Today, alumni are involved in virtually every area of the academic enterprise, participating in student recruitment and continuing education programs, serving on advisory committees, and helping to select presidents. Including alumni on university boards of trustees is now a common practice. J. L. Morrill of Ohio State University has pointed out that "the colleges and universities of this country have created the concept of alumni organization, loyalty, and support . . . and have developed that concept into a positive force in the social order, a powerful influence in the whole area of private philanthropy and a phenomenon well recognized in the area of practical pressure politics. The alumni in America, as in no other land, have helped build the institutions of higher learning by their interest, their gifts, and their organized sponsorship of state appropriations" (Turner, 1947, p. 3).

Alumni support institutions in many ways. As donors, they provide "extras for excellence" that colleges and universities cannot secure from other sources (the Council for Financial Aid to Education, 1985, reported that alumni gave more than $1 billion to higher education in 1983-84). As voters, they have significant influence in decisions affecting higher education. As parents, they affect their children's choice of institution and programs. And, as employers, they provide opportunities for internships and field studies and establish hiring and promotion criteria that affect the type of programs educational institutions offer.

The key to effective relations with alumni is promoting their deeper involvement in matters of concern to both them and their alma maters. More and more colleges are devoting funds and time to the development of student alumni clubs. Donald W. Griffin, for thirty years alumni secretary for Princeton University, stressed the importance of this by saying: "The first part of the alumni program begins on the campus. If four years are something vital to a student, he or she will become an active alumnus. . . . I got to know at least 100 undergraduates in every class. We invited six to breakfast every Sunday morning. We made offers of service to the class officers, gave them a place to meet in the alumni house. We helped student groups to travel. We pushed all the related services to try and let them know the alumni cared" (Rowland, 1977, p. 327). The publications annotated in this chapter will assist advancement practitioners in improving alumni relations in these and a variety of other ways.

References

Rowland, A. Westley (gen. ed.). *Handbook of Institutional Advancement: A Practical Guide to College and University Relations, Fund Raising, Alumni Relations, Government Relations, Publications, and Executive Management for Continued Advancement.* (1st ed.) San Francisco: Jossey-Bass, 1977.

Turner, F. H. *An Adventure in Alumni Relations.* Nashville, Tenn.: Vanderbilt University Press, 1947.

326 Alberger, Patricia L. (ed.). *Student Alumni Associations and Foundations.* Washington, D.C.: Council for Advancement and Support of Education, 1980. 65 pages.

The transformation of a graduate into a good alumnus requires hard work; this publication will help colleges and universities to work with students during their college years so that they will become effective alumni. It describes in detail how to involve students in alumni and fund-raising activities, covering benefits to the institution; getting started; budgeting, promotion, and programming; involving faculty, administration, and alumni; and using students in recruiting.

★**327** Alberger, Patricia L. (ed.). *How to Work Effectively with Alumni Boards.* Washington, D.C.: Council for Advancement and Support of Education, 1981. 81 pages.

This publication is recommended for advancement practitioners who want to improve their working relationships with alumni boards. Authors include suggestions by alumni board members, alumni administrators, professionals from CASE, and representatives of the Association of Governing Boards and the Association of Community College Trustees. The topics they address include leadership role of alumni boards, qualifications of board members, relationships between the institution's president and other administrators, and board involvement in various educational and institutional issues.

328 Barrett, Stephen (ed.). *Passport to Successful Alumni Travel Programs.* Washington, D.C.: Council for Advancement and Support of Education, 1983. 96 pages.

This publication covers what alumni travel can do for colleges and universities, how the law and the IRS affect travel programs, how to design, market, and promote travel programs, and how to ensure a rewarding experience for tour participants. It includes a travel glossary, a sample tour-host checklist, and a sample tour director's handbook. This material is especially valuable for alumni associations that have not yet developed travel programs.

329 Blakely, B. E. *Alumni Administration at State Colleges and Universities.* Washington, D.C.: Council for Advancement and Support of Education, 1979. 30 pages.

This report is the result of a nationwide survey of alumni directors at 132 state colleges and universities. Topics covered include job satisfaction, alumni directors' assessments of current issues in the conduct of alumni programs, changes taking place in the emphasis given to various aspects of the alumni program, and the use of CASE support services by members.

330 Carl, Linda. *The Alumni College Movement.* Washington, D.C.: Council for Advancement and Support of Education, 1977. 63 pages.

Based on the results of a nationwide survey of U.S. institutions offering alumni colleges, this work covers all aspects of alumni colleges, from history, sponsorship, format, and subject matter to noted successes and failures.

★331 Carter, Virginia L., and Alberger, Patricia L. *Building Your Alumni Program.* Washington, D.C.: Council for Advancement and Support of Education, 1980. 122 pages.

This spiral-bound collection features eighty of the best articles from *CASE Currents* on alumni involvement. Major sections describe managing the alumni association (principles and case studies), financing the association, involving students, activities and programs for alumni, chapters and clubs, continuing education, travel programs, record keeping, and working with alumni volunteers.

332 Council for Advancement and Support of Education. "Alumni Relations." *CASE Currents,* 1979, *5* (entire issue 5).

This special issue of *CASE Currents* deals with several important topics in alumni relations. Helpful articles include "Alumni Relations: Moving into the Mainstream"; "Are Alumni Clubs Important?"; "Your President: A Resource for Good Alumni Relations"; "Working with Alumni Boards"; "Attracting New Alumni Through Continuing Education"; "Financial Planning: A Must for Solvency"; "Getting into Externships"; "Add More Education to Your Travel Programs"; "Add Color to Reunions"; and "Should the Alumni Run the Annual Fund?"

333 Council for Advancement and Support of Education. "Alumni Periodicals." *CASE Currents,* 1980, *6* (entire issue 3).

This special issue of *CASE Currents* covers the whys and hows of preparing a good alumni periodical. Leading editors discuss how to deal with controversy, special issues, headlines and captions, and class notes. Other topics include photocommunication, layout, subscriptions and advertising, and the one-person shop.

334 Council for Advancement and Support of Education. "Alumni in Career Planning." *CASE Currents,* 1981, *7* (6), 8–18.

This issue of *CASE Currents* contains a special section on effective use of alumni in career planning. It offers suggestions on training graduates as career counselors, designing career-education workshops, alumni-sponsored student internships, and placement activities.

335 Council for Advancement and Support of Education. "Reunions." *CASE Currents*, 1984, *10* (entire issue 2).

The articles in this issue of *CASE Currents* focus on the importance of class reunions in developing esprit de corp among alumni. Most helpful is a listing of thirteen ways to make reunions work effectively (drawn from the results of a survey among alumni directors); an article by Edward Moore adds ten steps to a successful class reunion.

336 Council for Advancement and Support of Education. "Alumni Clubs." *CASE Currents*, 1985, *11* (entire issue 2).

Included in this special edition of *CASE Currents* are suggestions for developing winning alumni clubs (royal treatment for club leaders, providing important publications, handling mailings, providing services). It explains how to determine the cost effectiveness of alumni clubs, provides an analysis of Syracuse University's alumni program, and describes the development of an international club network.

337 Forman, Robert G. "Alumni Relations: Moving into the Mainstream." *CASE Currents*, 1979, *5* (5), 6-9.

In this article, part of an issue devoted exclusively to alumni relations (see entry number 332), the author traces the history of alumni relations from the first alumni association in 1821 to the present. He points out that the profession has moved through three phases: the organizational phase, when alumni relations progressed from offering merely social involvement to offering support for the alma mater; the program phase, which saw the development of a wide variety of programs and techniques for carrying them out; and the final phase, for which this article is subtitled—"Moving into the Mainstream." The author believes that, in the future the alumni relations office and its professionals must move from the background into the mainstream of efforts to safeguard the life of American colleges and universities.

338 Forman, Robert G. "Alumni Doesn't Just Spell Money." *CASE Currents*, 1984, *10* (8), 26–28.

In this article, Forman stresses that the primary objective of alumni relations is to develop programs that enable alumni to better serve their alma mater in a variety of ways, not just by giving money. He points to a largely overlooked role for alumni: participation in the decision-making processes of a university, in such areas as curriculum, entrance requirements, graduate requirements, and prerequisites.

339 Gorman, Brian (ed.). *Finding Lost Alumni: Tracing Methods Used by 19 Institutions*. Washington, D.C.: Council for Advancement and Support of Education, 1981. 30 pages.

Based on data from a nationwide survey, this book outlines techniques used by large and small institutions to trace and keep track of alumni. It includes sample postcards and questionnaires as well as articles on record keeping.

340 Ransdell, Gary A. (ed.). "Part Four: Alumni Administration: Building Institutional Support and Commitment." In A. Westley Rowland (gen. ed.), *Handbook of Institutional Advancement: A Practical Guide to College and University Relations, Fund Raising, Alumni Relations, Government Relations, Publications, and Executive Management for Continued Advancement*. (2nd ed.) San Francisco: Jossey-Bass, 1986. 122 pages.

This section of the *Handbook* discusses the mutual relationship between the institution and its alumni. Comprehensive selections cover management of alumni programs, governance, and constituent organizations, as well as the current issues surrounding nontraditional and continuing education, auxiliary programs and events, and the survey research that has contributed to a greater understanding of alumni relations in all settings. (For a description of the *Handbook* in its entirety, see entry number 54.)

341 Reichley, Robert A. "Part Three: Alumni Administration." In A. Westley Rowland (gen. ed.), *Handbook of Institutional Advancement: A Practical Guide to College and University Relations, Fund Raising, Alumni Relations, Government Relations, Publications, and Executive Management for Continued Advancement.* (1st ed.) San Francisco: Jossey-Bass, 1977. 63 pages.

The author of these chapters has long experience in working with alumni, and his coverage of the field is detailed and authoritative. The section covers almost every phase of alumni programming and administration—the use of volunteers, staffing, alumni clubs and reunions, student programs, and alumni publications—and includes useful suggestions from other alumni professionals. This work is recommended for new alumni staff people; it can also serve as a useful checklist for review by the experienced alumni administrator. (For a description of the *Handbook* in its entirety, see entry number 54.)

342 Spaeth, Joe L., and Greeley, Andrew M. *Recent Alumni and Higher Education.* Report prepared for the Carnegie Commission on Higher Education. New York: McGraw-Hill, 1974. 199 pages.

This book, which presents the results of a longitudinal study of 1961 college graduates, provides an analysis of alumni responses to questions concerning the goals of higher education, the college experience and culture, memories of the alma mater, reform of higher education, political and social attitudes, and the financial contributions of alumni to their former schools. The authors investigate the determinants of college entrance, the role of college in career planning, and the role of higher education in actual occupational attainment. The concluding chapter evaluates the importance of these findings to present educational policies and practices.

★**343** Williams, Dorothy F. (ed.). *Communicating with Alumni.* New Directions for Institutional Advancement, no. 4. San Francisco: Jossey-Bass, 1979. 120 pages.

This sourcebook describes methods for communicating effectively with the ever-expanding body of college and university graduates, including newsletters, newspapers, magazines, films, video and audio messages, and direct mail, with an emphasis on the communication vehicles themselves.

★**344** Zagoren, Adelaide M. (ed.). *Involving Alumni in Career Assistance Programs.* Washington, D.C.: Council for Advancement and Support of Education, 1981. 81 pages.

This is a detailed guide for organizing programs that will serve future graduates and involve current alumni in career-assistance programs. The author suggests that if an alumni program can provide tangible services to students, particularly career assistance, the institution has a better chance of maintaining their loyalty as alumni. The first part of the book explains how to set up a career-assistance program—services that can be offered, how to work with other campus offices, and how to keep accurate records. Part 2 consists of thirteen case studies describing how colleges, universities, and independent schools involve alumni in career days, job networks, counseling services, internships, and externships.

6

Government Relations

Government is inextricably intertwined with higher education, and every college and university, public or private, needs constantly to monitor its relationship with all levels of government. The importance of this relationship is underlined by the fact that many colleges and universities have established special staffs to work exclusively in this area. Some institutions have appointed a vice-president for government relations; in others, the position is called director of legislative relations. Whatever the name, colleges and universities have recognized this as an important area of institutional advancement and have moved aggressively to establish liaison with government.

The heart of this function is effective communication with government officials and their staffs at all levels concerning government policies that affect the welfare of colleges and universities. The publications annotated in this chapter will assist government liaison officers in carrying out this task. The works listed here discuss such crucial topics as public understanding of higher education, adequate funding, retirement, collective bargaining, tenure, affirmative action and equal opportunity, facilities for people with handicaps, research grants, sabbaticals, grievance procedures, and a whole array of other regulations and procedures established at every level of government.

345 Bailey, Stephen K. *Educational Interest Groups in the Nation's Capital.* Washington, D.C.: American Council on Education, 1975. 87 pages.

In this comprehensive summary of the 250–300 educational interest groups operating in Washington, Bailey tells us who they are, whom they represent, what they want, how they function, and what tasks they face. The book reports on ways in which these groups have been successful in the past and offers advice on what is needed for the future.

★**346** Berdahl, Robert O. *Statewide Coordination of Higher Education.* Washington, D.C.: American Council on Education, 1971. 285 pages.

This study of the emerging relations between higher education and state governments identifies the major source of friction in these relations as the conflict between university autonomy and public interest. The book describes the evolution of state coordinating boards for higher education and analyzes the structures, functions, and relationships of the various types of state coordinating agencies. It examines such issues as the impact of federal programs on state coordination and the relationship between state and private higher education. The author makes recommendations for easing the tensions in what he calls "the uneasy partnership" between the states and higher education.

★**347** Breneman, D. W., and Finn, C. E., Jr. (eds.). *Public Policy and Private Higher Education.* Washington, D.C.: Brookings Institution, 1978. 468 pages.

Chapters in this book deal with such specific issues as the federal tax policy, federal student aid policies, the economics of private higher education, the demand for private higher education, and state higher education policies. After reviewing the present state of private colleges and universities, the authors conclude that if existing state and federal government policies toward private higher education are not altered, private educational institutions will continue to deteriorate. They present alternatives to this situation, with recommendations that blend economic and political perspectives, such as stabilizing and narrowing the tuition gap between private and public higher education and helping students bridge the gap through government aid programs.

★**348** Carnegie Foundation for the Advancement of Teaching. *The States and Higher Education: A Proud Past and a Vital Future.* San Francisco: Jossey-Bass, 1976. 94 pages.

This book discusses the interrelationships between the states and higher education. Part 1 examines the performance of the states and discusses such major policy issues as improving coordination, assuring institutional independence, maintaining dynamism without growth, determining parochialism, and preserving private institutions. Part 2 examines diversity in state programs in terms of practices, patterns of campus governance, and state coordination. Twenty-nine tables illustrate the findings and provide state-by-state data for comparisons.

349 Congressional Staff Directory. *1985 C.S.D. Advance Locator.* Mount Vernon, Va.: Congressional Staff Directory, 1985. 468 pages.

Often referred to as "the Bible for the Hill," this publication contains biographies of 3,200 top congressional staffers, enabling advancement professionals who work in the area of government relations to update their files on members of Congress, their staffs, and their districts. Included are a handy ten-page index of members with new suite and telephone numbers, listings of state delegations, 9,900 cities, and staffs of the senators and representatives, and an individual index. The work is updated annually.

350 Congressional Staff Directory. *1986 Congressional Staff Directory.* (28th ed.) Mount Vernon, Va.: Congressional Staff Directory, 1986. 1,232 pages.

This directory, updated annually, provides detailed information on the staffs of members of Congress and their assignments to committees and subcommittees. A key-word subject index includes listings by individual, subcommittee, bureau, caucus, commission, department, and agency. The work contains biographies of 3,200 staff members and an update on key personnel in the executive branch.

351 Congressional Staff Directory. *1986 Federal Staff Directory.* (5th ed.) Mount Vernon, Va.: Congressional Staff Directory, 1986. 1,344 pages.

This directory provides listings of 28,000 executive-branch staff members, with job titles, buildings, rooms, and phone extensions, and contains biographies of 2,200 key executives. Entries include top policy advisers, White House staff, cabinet-level department members, independent-agency executives, ambassadors, attorneys, and freedom-of-information contacts. Listings are indexed by subject key word and individual name. The directory is updated annually.

352 Council for Advancement and Support of Education. "State Relations." *CASE Currents,* 1981, 7 (entire issue 1).

This special issue of *CASE Currents,* devoted to state legislative relations, provides tips on lobbying, working with state legislators, using volunteers, and the effective legislative relations team.

353 Crawford, Edwin M. (ed.). "Part Four: Government Relations." In A. Westley Rowland (gen. ed.), *Handbook of Institutional Advancement: A Practical Guide to College and University Relations, Fund Raising, Alumni Relations, Government Relations, Publications, and Executive Management for Continued Advancement.* (1st ed.) San Francisco: Jossey-Bass, 1977. 48 pages.

This selection includes four chapters on effective government relations within the context of institutional advancement. Crawford's overview offers advice on the operations of government relations offices. The remaining chapters cover the principles of effective government relations, state and local relations, and relations with the federal government. (For a description of the *Handbook* in its entirety, see entry number 54.)

★**354** Finn, Chester. *Scholars, Dollars, and Bureaucrats.* Washington, D.C.: Brookings Institution, 1978. 238 pages.

In this book, Finn competently analyzes the various dimensions of federal involvement in higher education, covering student aid programs, research grants, and affirmative action activities. He also discusses the issues surrounding the creation of a separate federal Department of Education.

355 Folger, John K. (ed.). *Increasing the Public Accountability of Higher Education.* New Directions for Institutional Research, no. 16. San Francisco: Jossey-Bass, 1977. 99 pages.

In response to a desire to increase accountability of institutions of higher education, many states have begun looking beyond fiscal standards and have become concerned with whether institutions are doing an effective job and using their resources wisely. This book examines various approaches that have been used to improve this situation, such as performance budgeting, performance audits, and program reviews.

356 Hook, Sidney, Kurtz, Paul, and Todorovich, Miro (eds.). *The University and the State.* Buffalo, N.Y.: Prometheus, 1978. 296 pages.

This work is a collection of essays first delivered at the fourth general meeting of University Centers for Rational Alternatives, held in 1976. The articles address the nature of the universities' relationships with state and federal government. Topics include government regulation and academic freedom, the costs to colleges and universities of implementing federally mandated social programs, and the interaction of state and federal policy.

357 Hughes, John F. (ed.). *Education and the State*. Washington, D.C.: American Council on Education, 1975. 275 pages.

This book outlines eight areas of concern regarding the interrelationships between higher education and government. It includes selections on setting national goals and objectives; financing; coordinating federal, state, and institutional decisions; the management systems approach; educational reform and innovation; the faculty and the government; and legislating attitudes. A number of suggestions for increasing effective cooperation between higher education and government are offered.

★**358** Johnson, Marvin D. (ed.). *Successful Governmental Relations*. New Directions for Institutional Advancement, no. 12. San Francisco: Jossey-Bass, 1981. 97 pages.

This sourcebook offers a guide to the development of a successful government relations program or the improvement of an existing one. It recommends ways to use trustees, presidents, lobbyists, community leaders, national associations, and the news media to increase and improve higher education's representation in government.

359 Kennedy, Richard L. "Part Five: Improving Government Relations." In A. Westley Rowland (gen. ed.), *Handbook of Institutional Advancement: A Practical Guide to College and University Relations, Fund Raising, Alumni Relations, Government Relations, Publications, and Executive Management for Continued Advancement*. (2nd ed.) San Francisco: Jossey-Bass, 1986. 36 pages.

Government involvement in educational institutions has led to the need for administrative mechanisms that can effectively manage the relationships between the two. This part of the *Handbook* speaks to the development of policy and decision-making processes for institutional officers and issues of concern surrounding funding and legislative actions at all levels and in different academic settings. Kennedy makes the case that government relations is one of the most critical external interfaces in higher education today, requiring careful attention to planning and deployment of resources. (For a description of the *Handbook* in its entirety, see entry number 54.)

360 Millard, Richard. *State Boards of Higher Education.* Washington, D.C.: U.S. Department of Health, Education, and Welfare, Office of Education, 1974. 69 pages.

This report summarizes the historical development of statewide higher education boards and describes their functions, powers, and legal structures. Particularly useful is the discussion on the evolution of federally supported state 1202 commissions.

361 Miller, Robert A. (ed.). *The Federal Role in Education: New Directions for the Eighties.* Washington, D.C.: Institute for Educational Leadership, 1981. 187 pages.

This work is a collection of essays speculating on the future of the federal role in education. While primarily concerned with elementary and secondary education, these discussions on how federal policy is formed, how federal and state governments interact, and federal participation in educational financing are also relevant to higher education.

362 Millett, John D. *Conflict in Higher Education: State Government Coordination Versus Institutional Independence.* San Francisco: Jossey-Bass, 1984. 285 pages.

This book focuses on how state governments regulate, finance, and coordinate higher education in twenty-five states. It describes the role and activities of statewide governing boards, coordinating boards, and advisory boards and discusses how pressures on these often lead to conflicts between educators and administrators. The author also examines ways in which academic leaders can work to improve cooperation with boards while achieving greater autonomy in governance.

363 Seabury, Paul (ed.). *Bureaucrats and Brainpower: Government Regulation of Universities.* San Francisco: Institute for Contemporary Studies, 1979. 150 pages.

This book discusses the relationship between universities and the government. A chapter by Richard W. Lyman, former president of Stanford University, provides an inside look at how federal government regulations affected Stanford and how that institution responded. Six strategies are suggested: learn how regulatory policy is established and how to influence it, teach and do research on federal regulation, make political alliances with other interest groups, avoid overreacting, know when not to compromise, and be willing to say no to certain programs.

364 Speich, Don F., and Weiner, Stephen S. *In the Eye of the Storm: Proposition 13 and Public Education in California.* Washington, D.C.: Institute for Educational Leadership, 1980. 104 pages.

This publication discusses the impact on education of a tax-cutting proposition in California. It describes how the proposition was passed, how the legislature bailed out education and local government, and how the proposition has affected public services in general and education in particular. The authors examine the implications of the California experience for other states.

365 U.S. Government Printing Office. *United States Government Manual 1984–85.* Washington, D.C.: U.S. Government Printing Office, 1985.

This official handbook of the federal government describes every federal department, agency, and commission, as well as quasi-governmental organizations. It includes agency addresses, key personnel, and phone numbers and is updated annually.

7

Publications

At the heart of institutional advancement is communication, and publications are among the most effective communication tools. Publications play a vital role in interpreting an institution to its publics. Whether viewed from the standpoint of money spent, people contacted, or quantity issued, publications are a basic and important part of a modern and dynamic institutional advancement program.

Probably the first publication from a college or university in this country was *New England's First Fruits,* a pamphlet designed to raise funds for Harvard College. Since that time, publications have evolved in response to a need for support of the many other functions of advancement as well. When colleges and universities needed a system for listing and publishing their course offerings, the college catalogue developed. When alumni needed information about their alma maters, newsletters and magazines were issued. As fund-raising programs became more complex and sophisticated, they demanded a wide variety of brochures and reports. When student-recruitment and advancement professionals recognized their common interests, they joined to produce student-recruitment literature as well as a variety of career-oriented publications. When government relations, a recent development in advancement activities, became an important program for colleges and universities, it required support in the form of newsletters and reports for every level of government. This need-response pattern can be seen in every area of advancement activities.

Each year, colleges and universities issue millions of printed pieces directed at specific publics of importance to them, including catalogues, newsletters, handbooks, magazines, reports, brochures, posters, directories, guidance and career booklets, recruitment materials, programs, and books. These publications represent one of the largest items in the budgets of advancement officers, with millions of dollars spent for printing alone. The role of publications in the total institutional advancement program takes on additional importance when their unique function is considered: while many aspects of advancement are impersonal or abstract, a publication is concrete—something that can be held in one's hand, something that seems to convey a personal message from the institution. To many who are not intimately acquainted with an institution, a publication *is* the institution.

Whether catalogues, annual reports, or simple departmental brochures, publications mirror what an institution is, what it stands for, and what it believes in; they reflect its personality and create an image for its publics. The guidelines listed below are important in ensuring that an institution's publications most effectively reflect the desired image.

Publications must accurately reflect the excellence of an institution. The mirror must not distort the true image of the college or university. Publications must not falsify the facts of campus beauty, faculty stature, curriculum diversity, architectural style, or the variety of extracurricular activities available (too often described as the "best in the land"). Integrity, dignity, and true dedication to the purposes of education are essential; a publication presenting a picture that is not justified by fact may eventually become a liability.

Publications must be as free of errors as possible. Grammar, punctuation, writing style, readability, design, choice of type and paper, and proofreading must be of the very best. This quality is expected of an educational institution; anything less destroys the image of excellence.

Publications should be handled by professionals. Effective publications require people experienced in graphic arts; they cannot be produced by amateurs. (As an aside, there is much room for colleges and universities to promote training in graphic arts for higher education, an area inadequately covered at present.)

An effective publications program requires comprehensive planning and organization, sufficient personnel, and an adequate budget. Organization of publications programs in colleges and universities varies widely. Some institutions have no organization at all or have completely decentralized operations, with each unit of the institution making its own decisions regarding content, design, and budget. At institutions with publications departments, the use of such a department's services may be optional. The most effective type of organization is an integrated system, with all publications routed through a central publications office with fixed responsibility for the institution's entire publications program. This type of system allows for standardized production procedures for optimal economy and efficiency and the highest standards of excellence.

Content is the first test of quality. Publications must say something important—and say it well. Other aspects of publications—design, type choice, selection of paper, use of color—are important insofar as they help relay the content to the reader and themselves create an impression, but a publication without good content is not worth printing.

The works annotated in this chapter have been selected to assist advancement practitioners in meeting these standards in their institutions' publications.

General

★**366** Arden, Kelvin, and Whalen, William J. *Effective Publications for Colleges and Universities.* (Rev. ed.) Washington, D.C.: Council for Advancement and Support of Education, 1978. 180 pages.

This comprehensive study of a successful publications program is full of practical information. It explains how to organize the office and staff, buy printing, edit copy, and use art and photography. In addition, the authors give twenty-six ideas for stretching your publications dollar. Chapters deal with special publications, such as annual reports, catalogues, and faculty-staff newsletters; fund-raising publications; handbooks for faculty, students, and others;

and the new technology and how it affects graphic communication. A special section discusses direct mail, including its use in fund raising. Also included are a sample style manual, a bibliography, and assorted checklists.

367 Arth, Marvin, and Ashmore, Helen. *Newsletter Editor's Deskbook.* Portland, Oreg.: Coast to Coast Books, 1983. 216 pages.

This publication offers a concise review of journalism principles as they are applied to special-audience periodicals, such as newsletters, magazines, and newspapers. It focuses on how to find news, judge it, and write about it, offering help with questions of legality, objectivity, and credibility and suggestions for working with reporters.

368 Bennett, Ann Granning (ed.). "Part Six: Publications: The Vital Link to Constituencies." In A. Westley Rowland (gen. ed.), *Handbook of Institutional Advancement: A Practical Guide to College and University Relations, Fund Raising, Alumni Relations, Government Relations, Publications, and Executive Management for Continued Advancement.* (2nd ed.) San Francisco: Jossey-Bass, 1986. 58 pages.

This section of the *Handbook* addresses the fact that publications reach the largest audience of an institution and are one of the most effective means for delivering meaningful messages. Chapters discuss writing, designing, and producing winning publications for general and specific audiences and cover planning objectives, networking, and managing publications overall. (For a description of the *Handbook* in its entirety, see entry number 54.)

★369 Carter, Virginia L. (ed.). *Developing a Publications Policy.* Washington, D.C.: Council for Advancement and Support of Education, 1978. 96 pages (microfiche).

This publication presents the results of a survey of university policies regarding publications at a number of institutions in the western United States. It includes copies of the institutions' individual publication policies.

370 Carter, Virginia L. (ed.). *Update on Publications.* Washington, D.C.: Council for Advancement and Support of Education, 1978. 192 pages plus eight tapes.

This is an audio-print career-development kit for those working in publications. It includes Arden and Whalen's *Effective Publications for Colleges and Universities* (see entry number 366). Eight audio tapes deal with writing, developing print specifications, managing small and large shops, working with designers, saving money on publications, and understanding the new technologies.

371 Carter, Virginia L., and Alberger, Patricia LaSalle (eds.). *How to Cut Publications Costs.* (Rev. ed.) Washington, D.C.: Council for Advancement and Support of Education, 1984. 98 pages.

This work covers both general approaches and specific tips for maximizing every dollar spent on publications. Chapters range from computer typesetting to using a quick-print center.

372 Chickering, Robert B., and Hartman, Susan. *How to Register a Copyright and Protect Your Creative Work.* New York: Scribner's, 1980. 26 pages.

This basic guide to the new copyright law provides a step-by-step review of how to protect a copyright. It explains what works can and cannot be copyrighted; how to register a claim; how long copyright lasts and how to renew it; and what constitutes proper copyright notice. It also discusses a number of special situations and exceptions for nonprofit and religious uses. Appendixes include a summary of the major changes in the law, a review of other forms of protection, and a listing of information sources.

373 Crawford, Anne R. (ed.). "Part Five: Publications." In A. Westley Rowland (gen. ed.), *Handbook of Institutional Advancement: A Practical Guide to College and University Relations, Fund Raising, Alumni Relations, Government Relations, Publications, and Executive Management for Continued Advancement.* (1st ed.) San Francisco: Jossey-Bass, 1977. 52 pages.

In the first edition of the *Handbook,* this section consists of five chapters dealing with such topics as organization of the publications office, researching the market, production of publications, techniques and devices to cut costs, and publications for key audiences. (For a description of the *Handbook* in its entirety, see entry number 54.)

374 Johnston, Donald F. *Copyright Handbook.* New York: Bowker, 1978. 309 pages.

This book explains the new copyright law and its complexities, discussing the similarities and differences between the old and the new laws. Among the many topics treated are copyrightable subject matter, copyright notices, registration, infringement remedies, duration of copyright, and fair use.

375 Newspaper Enterprise Association. *The World Almanac and Book of Facts.* New York: Newspaper Enterprise Association, 1985. 976 pages.

This book, published annually, is an indispensable tool for advancement practitioners, providing the latest statistical data in almost every area. First published in 1868, it has continued to sell widely to writers, editors, speech writers, and others.

376 University of Chicago Press. *The Chicago Manual of Style.* (13th ed.) Chicago: University of Chicago Press, 1969. 738 pages.

For over seventy-five years, the University of Chicago Press's *Manual of Style* has been the standard reference tool for authors, editors, copywriters, and proofreaders. It has been updated many times since 1906; the thirteenth edition, the first revision since 1969, also introduced the book's first change in title. The first part of the *Manual* discusses the fundamentals of bookmaking, including manuscript preparation and permissions and copyright information. Part 2, the core of the book, is concerned with matters of style that most often perplex both author and editor. The third part deals with the actual production and printing of a book, providing helpful information on design and typography and an extensive glossary of technical terms. This revised edition reflects the impact of the new technology on the entire editing and publishing process, discusses the changes in the copyright laws, and offers greater detail on the procedures with which it deals.

377 Volkmann, M. Fredric. "Printing Specifications: Writing Them Right." *CASE Currents*, 1984, *10*, 54–59.

The author of this article shares his many years of printing experience with the reader, presenting the essentials for developing printing specifications to produce a quality publication. He suggests that the first step is to determine quantity, budget, content, audience, means of distribution, and deadlines and illustrates his article with a sample planning guide for recording information on suppliers—equipment, capabilities, and reputation for quality. A model printing-specifications form is included.

Periodicals

378 Gillespie, Maralyn Orbison (ed.). "Part Seven: Periodicals: Formats, Uses, and Financial Strategies." In A. Westley Rowland (gen. ed.), *Handbook of Institutional Advancement: A Practical Guide to College and University Relations, Fund Raising, Alumni Relations, Government Relations, Publications, and Executive Management for Continued Advancement.* (2nd ed.) San Francisco: Jossey-Bass, 1986. 54 pages.

Based on the premise that the periodical is the most powerful means of sharing important information with the greatest number of people, the selections in this section speak to the pleasures and pitfalls of planning and producing quality magazines that put forth positive impressions of the institution. Chapters cover alumni, internal, and special-purpose periodicals and the kinds of news items that are most effective for each. They include many useful hints and insights from people experienced in the art of enhancing communication through the design and distribution of periodicals. (For a description of the *Handbook* in its entirety, see entry number 54.)

379 Hudson, Howard Penn. *Publishing Newsletters.* Portland, Oreg.: Coast to Coast Books, 1982. 224 pages.

This book is a goldmine of sound advice on such topics as market analysis, editorial planning, use of direct mail, and business management. It is especially helpful for the editor trying to build circulation through direct-mail advertising.

380 Kacmarczyk, Ronald, and Rickes, Persis. *The Complete College Catalog Book.* Washington, D.C.: Council for Advancement and Support of Education, 1984. 88 pages.

This work provides a systematic and comprehensive approach to creating the college catalogue. It explains what should be included in the catalogue, efficient methods of collecting the information, and how to determine an institution's image, define its constituencies, improve writing, and cut production costs.

381 Public Relations Quarterly. *The Newsletter Yearbook Directory.* (5th ed.) Rhinebeck, N.Y.: Public Relations Quarterly, 1985. 324 pages.

This valuable reference covering the newsletter field includes a directory of 2,721 subscription newsletters, a history of modern newsletters, and a bibliography of the literature on newsletters. Entries include publishing company, key contacts, subscription information, and information on submitting press releases. Indexed by subject, geographical location, and name, it also includes a section with names, addresses, phone numbers, and contact people for over one hundred major suppliers. It is useful for both newcomers and those looking for new publicity outlets.

382 Smith, Cortland Gary. *The Right Content.* Plandome, N.Y.: Cortland Gary Smith, 1979. 220 pages.

This straightforward handbook for beginning periodical editors deals with the day-to-day problems of selecting editorial content, with an emphasis on employee, public relations, and association publications and publications supported by advertising or readers. Smith stresses that publications must satisfy both the sponsor and the reader and is a strong advocate for reader surveys. The book includes many handy examples of worksheets and schedules and a list of reader-survey services.

Editing

383 Beach, Mark. *Editing Your Newsletter: A Guide to Writing, Design, and Production.* (2nd ed.) Portland, Oreg.: Coast to Coast Books, 1984. 128 pages.

A complete guide to every step of newsletter production, from setting goals to getting distributed, this book provides instruction on specific techniques related to such aspects of the editor's job as selecting paper and print styles, composing a masthead, interviewing and working with reporters, and maintaining address lists. It discusses copyright law, developing story ideas, and using a word processor, as well as research on reader interests. It contains reproductions of eighty-five actual newsletters and nameplates; appendixes include sample forms, recommended reading, and the names and addresses of newsletters and editors' associations.

★384 Flint, Emily P. (ed.). *Creative Editing and Writing Workbook.* Washington, D.C.: Council for Advancement and Support of Education, 1979. 279 pages.

This workbook contains a comprehensive collection of articles on periodical editing, with a series of editing and writing exercises that can be used to sharpen skills or to conduct staff workshops.

The articles discuss such topics as editing and freedom of the press, tips on creative editing, writing for the educated reader, science writing and editing, artful interviewing, skillful news writing, use of humor and style, and writing persuasively for prospective students and alumni donors.

385 Judd, Karen. *Copyediting: A Practical Guide*. Los Altos, Calif.: Kaufmann, 1982. 287 pages.

This work is intended as a tool for all those who are involved in copyediting. It covers such topics as the nature of copyediting; punctuation and grammar; spelling, capitalization, and hyphenation; style and word usage; numbers and abbreviations; notes and bibliography; and type marking and keying.

Style, Design, and Graphics

386 Angione, Howard. *The Associated Press Stylebook*. (Rev. ed.) Dayton, Ohio: Lorenz Press, 1985. 296 pages.

This stylebook is a guide to capitalization, abbreviation, spelling and use of numerals, explaining special Associated Press usage. It is one of the standard works in the field.

387 Council for Advancement and Support of Education. "Publication Graphics." *CASE Currents*, 1982, *8* (entire issue 2).

This *CASE Currents* issue focuses on ways to improve publications design. It gives the inside story on how designers approach their tasks and includes samples of their work. It discusses the use of coordinated graphics to achieve institutional identity, describes "new wave" design, and explains how to buy four-color printing.

388 Council for Advancement and Support of Education. *Fund-Raising Fantasia.* Washington, D.C.: Council for Advancement and Support of Education, 1983. 25 illustrations.

This package contains twenty-five line drawings that combine old engravings with new concepts. It contains a potpourri of ideas and illustrations that may be used in fund-raising and promotional mailings, publications, and advertising materials.

389 Gerlach, Cameron. *Alumni Illustrations.* Washington, D.C.: Council for Advancement and Support of Education, 1977. 12 pages.

This work contains twenty line drawings illustrating various facets of alumni-institutional relationships, including homecomings and reunions, travel, continuing education, student counseling, sports, and fund raising. The drawings can be used in catalogues, newsletters, information flyers, and so on.

390 Helmken, Charles M. *Creative Newsletter Graphics.* (3rd ed.) Washington, D.C.: Council for Advancement and Support of Education, 1981. 280 pages.

This comprehensive workbook covers all aspects of newsletter design. It includes information on nameplate selection, how to work with a grid, and design concepts and the reasons behind them and contains thirty-nine type selections and twenty-three usable formats designed by top professionals, with a discussion and analysis of each format.

391 Helmken, Charles M. (ed.). *Creativity Illustrated.* Washington, D.C.: Council for Advancement and Support of Education, 1983. 182 pages.

This combination workbook and compendium provides access to just about any illustration needed for publication design. It lists 101 publications on illustrations, 101 sources of special kinds of illustrations, and 101 collections of clip art and includes 101 examples of contemporary illustrations and old prints used by colleges and universities and 606 ready-to-use, copyright-free engravings from the vast collection of Carl Herrman.

392 Helmken, Charles M. (ed.). *Potpourri Art Package.* Washington, D.C.: Council for Advancement and Support of Education, 1983. 24 pages.

This is a selection of 101 of the best illustrations taken from the *Creative Communications* art packages over the past ten years. Illustrations include symbols, sports, academics, students, faculty, border art, poster art, money items, and other useful subjects. Illustrations are camera ready and can be reduced or enlarged and printed in either one or two colors.

393 Helmken, Charles M. "Pop Goes the Poster!" *CASE Currents,* 1984, *10* (8), 40–43.

Colleges and universities make extensive use of posters, and advancement professionals are involved in both the design and production of these visual aids. Helmken contends that posters are clues to culture and that they persuade most successfully when message and graphics are happily married. He discusses several design and technique principles: symbolism, symbiosis, substitution, sequence, scale, silhouette, script, spectrum, and simplicity. He also suggests some things to avoid: typographical fog, color confusion, excessive elements, and poor placement. This is an excellent article for designers and publications editors.

394 International Paper Company. *Pocket Pal: A Graphic Arts Production Handbook.* (13th ed.) Portland, Oreg.: Coast to Coast Books, 1983. 216 pages.

Covering everything you need to know about the printing process, including press sizes, trade practices, inks, and papers, this classic book will help you increase printing quality and cut costs.

395 Jordan, Lewis (ed.). *The New York Times Manual of Style and Usage.* (Rev. ed.) New York: Quadrangle, 1976. 231 pages.

Used by *New York Times* editors and writers, this stylebook offers advice on spelling, punctuation, English usage, and overall writing quality. Guidelines on basic aspects of journalistic responsibility and explanations of weights and measures and terms in the arts and sciences are also included. The stylebook is arranged alphabetically for easy use.

396 Lem, Dean Philip. *Graphics Master 2.* Los Angeles: Dean Lem Associates, 1981. 36 pages.

A working handbook for anyone in the business of designing or producing printed materials, this book deals with such topics as printing processes, photomechanics, halftones, special-effect screens, process color, color correction, stripping and imposition, proofing methods, printing presses, typography, binding and finishing, and printing papers and envelopes. It includes a comprehensive graphic arts glossary; a process-color selection guide containing over 2,800 different colors; a typeface selector guide with 832 typeface specimens; a chart that converts lowercase alpha lengths into character-count key numbers; and presentations of the alphabet in 276 machine-set typefaces.

397 Lucas, Geir. *Student Package.* Washington, D.C.: Council for Advancement and Support of Education, 1978. 14 pages.

This is a package of twenty-five line illustrations showing students in various academic activities, including study, research, language lab, arts, sciences, and communications.

398 MacGregor, A. J. *Graphics Simplified.* Buffalo, N.Y.: University of Toronto Press, 1982. 64 pages.

This booklet tells the reader how to plan and prepare effective charts, graphs, illustrations, and other visual aids. It includes useful sections on specifications and includes designers' tools and aids.

399 Minor, Susan. *Faces of Education.* Washington, D.C.: Council for Advancement and Support of Education, 1981. 15 pages.

This is a collection of thirty original illustrations depicting women, minorities, and handicapped persons on campus. The black-and-white illustrations may be used as they are, or color can be added for effectiveness in catalogues, view books, promotional pieces, advertising, and posters.

400 Nelson, Roy Paul. *Publication Design.* (3rd ed.) Boston: Little, Brown, 1983. 320 pages.

This book shows how to combine art and photography to make publications readable and visually exciting.

401 Rappaport, Rick. "How to Bring Your Publication's Photography to Life." *CASE Currents,* 1984, *10* (4), 8–13.

In this illustrated article showing some good photographs, the author recommends that the photographer determine whether there is a center of interest in the image, avoid placing the center of interest in the center, eliminate distracting backgrounds, use dark or black backgrounds, hold the viewer's eye by keeping light tones away from the edges of the image, use out-of-focus foregrounds, use diagonal visual lines, make the subject's eye the center of interest, include repeating patterns of tone and shape, and observe the quality of light. The author suggests two good references: *The Camera,* TIME-LIFE Library of Photography, and *The Book of Photography* by John Hedgcoe from Random House.

402 Sanders, Norman. *Photographing for Publications.* Portland, Oreg.: Coast to Coast Books, 1983. 111 pages.

Written by a printer, this book explains how the lithograph process works to reproduce photographs and clearly describes techniques for producing the best possible photographs. It explains screens, halftones, and color separations and provides information on controlling the cost and quality of photographs.

403 White, Jan V. *Designing for Magazines.* New York: Bowker, 1982. 224 pages.

This publication examines the common problems editors have with front covers, editorial pages, feature-section coverage, and late-closing news. It offers realistic solutions to difficult problems.

404 White, Jan V. *Mastering Graphics: Design and Production Made Easy.* New York: Bowker, 1983. 180 pages.

This work presents a practical approach to the use of graphics as a tool for communication. Chapters discuss effective typography, illustrations and their substitutes, use of color, and commonsense solutions to everyday production problems.

8

Enrollment Management

Though advancement professionals have long dealt with many aspects of enrollment management—recruitment, retention, and replacement of students, institutional research, admissions and registration, and financial aid—student recruitment was not a major concern during times of rapidly expanding enrollments, and only a few institutions devoted much effort to this area. Now, in times of demographic change and declining enrollments, student recruitment has become of vital interest to colleges and universities.

Student recruitment has much in common with other areas of advancement. Meeting and corresponding with prospective students and their parents, designing recruitment literature to be of maximum usefulness to them, and similar activities are common to both the enrollment manager and the advancement officer. Because prospective students and their parents, guidance counselors, and high school principals are prime audiences for the advancement professional, some institutions have made enrollment management a separate department within the advancement program. Whatever the system, the advancement officer must work closely with the admissions office, the registrar, and the director of student aid.

To carry out this function effectively, advancement and enrollment officers must ask themselves such questions as these: What image of our institution is held by prospective students, their parents, and their high school counselors? Are we recruiting the quality and number of students that we want? Why do students choose to enroll at our institution—or choose not to? Why do students leave it? How are we doing in comparison with our competition? Is our tuition set at the right level? These and other questions relating to enrollment management are addressed in the publications annotated in this chapter.

★405 Alberger, Patricia L. *How to Involve Alumni in Student Recruitment.* Washington, D.C.: Council for Advancement and Support of Education, 1983. 84 pages.

This publication provides instructions on how to use alumni to increase an institution's applicant pool and attract students. It includes materials on starting a program, setting objectives, managing the program, coordinating it with the admissions office, and working with volunteers. An extensive appendix of sample materials includes newsletters, promotional pieces, and training materials.

406 Astin, Alexander W. *Preventing Students from Dropping Out.* San Francisco: Jossey-Bass, 1975. 204 pages.

This book reports the results of a nationwide survey of undergraduate students at 358 two-year colleges, four-year colleges, and universities—the first longitudinal multi-institutional study of college dropouts. The book provides information on student characteristics that predict dropping out (academic ability, family background, and so on) and shows how these are related to institutional characteristics such as size, cost, and location. The author discusses how policies regarding financial aid, employment, and student services can minimize the dropout rate and help students to stay in college.

407 Astin, Alexander W. *Four Critical Years: Effects of College on Beliefs, Attitudes, and Knowledge.* San Francisco: Jossey-Bass, 1977. 293 pages.

For a full description of this work, see entry number 36.

408 Beal, Philip E., and Noel, Lee. *What Works in Student Retention.* Iowa City, Iowa: American College Testing Program, 1980. 135 pages.

This report focuses on how students can be encouraged to stay in college. The author suggests a broad range of actions that institutions can take to increase retention, describing the effects of such variables as orientation programs, counseling, and financial aid.

409 Breneman, David W. *The Coming Enrollment Crisis: What Every Trustee Must Know.* Washington, D.C.: Association of Governing Boards of Universities and Colleges, 1982. 40 pages.

This brief but powerful work is an important study that can help trustees prepare for the future of their institutions. It contains over fifty projection charts providing state-by-state information about enrollment prospects from the present to the mid 1990s.

410 Carnegie Council on Policy Studies in Higher Education. *Fair Practices in Higher Education: Rights and Responsibilities of Students and Their Colleges in a Period of Intensified Competition for Enrollments.* San Francisco: Jossey-Bass, 1979. 91 pages.

In response to the growing consumer movement, the comparative scarcity of traditional-age students, and some negative aspects of higher education's conduct, the Carnegie Council commissioned this report, which focuses on the need for institutions to develop a code of rights and responsibilities that address such subjects as admissions, recruiting, advertising, financial aid, tuition, and advisement. The book makes fourteen general recommendations, some of which contain specific recommendations, concerning such topics as provision of better information for students and their parents, and adoption of a policy of institutional full disclosure.

411 Carnegie Council on Policy Studies in Higher Education. *The Next Step for the 1980s in Student Financial Aid: A Fourth Alternative.* San Francisco: Jossey-Bass, 1979. 255 pages.

This report was published to coincide with the 1979 review of the Higher Education Act. It examines the current system of student financial aid, discusses opportunities for improvement, and makes a specific recommendation (the fourth alternative), which calls for a major overhaul of existing programs in order to make them more equitable in their impact, more solid in their administration, and more cost efficient.

★**412** Chapman, David W. (ed.). *Improving College Information for Prospective Students.* Washington, D.C.: Council for Advancement and Support of Education, 1980. 128 pages.

This volume explains how to develop publications that tell students what they want and need to know about an institution. It outlines ways to improve information about academic programs, costs and financial aid available, and college services offered. It also describes ways to measure and report the educational and employment outcomes of an institution's academic programs and includes a helpful checklist for evaluating a college's recruitment literature.

413 College Entrance Examination Board. *A Role for Marketing in College Admissions.* New York: College Entrance Examination Board, 1976. 113 pages.

This publication discusses the application of marketing theories and practices to college admissions. It covers such topics as assessing consumer needs and informing prospective students of what the college has to offer and makes suggestions for future planning in response to changing consumer needs.

414 Council for Advancement and Support of Education. "Student Recruitment." *CASE Currents,* 1980, *6* (11), 8–34.

In this special insert to *CASE Currents* on recruiting students, feature articles discuss the recruiting of adult students and two-year college graduates as well as providing information on advertising and increasing applicant pools.

415 Council for Advancement and Support of Education. "The Personal Touch in Student Recruitment." *CASE Currents*, 1985, *11* (entire issue 4).

This special issue of *Case Currents* covers effective methods for student recruitment. In one article, eight students tell what really influenced their college decisions; another describes how a large university can "get personal in a crowd." Other topics include how a campus visit can give students a first-hand look and how to use students in student recruitment.

★416 Henry, Joe B. (ed.). *The Impact of Student Financial Aid on Institutions.* New Directions for Institutional Research, no. 25. San Francisco: Jossey-Bass, 1980. 110 pages.

This sourcebook provides an analysis of the present and potential impact of student aid programs, policies, and procedures on institutions and their students. It addresses the major issues in need of resolution and suggests practical steps that can be taken for more effective management of aid programs. Especially relevant are chapters on planning by R. Bacchetti, on market management by W. I. Elliott, and on student aid and student need by D. Pacher.

★417 Hossler, Don. *Enrollment Management: An Integrated Approach.* New York: College Entrance Examination Board, 1984. 167 pages.

This book provides an in-depth look at the expanding role of today's admissions professionals and how they are having an increasing impact on institutional policy making at the highest levels. The author carefully examines enrollment management, a process that influences the size, shape, and characteristics of a student body by directing student marketing and recruitment, as well as pricing and financial aid. Additionally, this study describes the influential positions of enrollment managers regarding academic and career advisement, academic assistance programs, institutional research, orientation and retention programs, and student services. This important study discusses the demand for higher education, college choice, pricing and financial aid, recruiting graduates, retaining students, the impact of college on students, the outcomes of higher education, and the future of enrollment management.

418 Ihlanfeldt, William. *Achieving Optimal Enrollments and Tuition Revenues: A Guide to Modern Methods of Market Research, Student Recruitment, and Institutional Pricing.* San Francisco: Jossey-Bass, 1980. 267 pages.

This is a how-to-do-it guide to the practices of marketing, including the possibilities for alternative tuition pricing systems. Topics include how to design and conduct market research, plan the marketing effort, implement and evaluate market strategies, and improve promotional communications overall.

419 Maguire, John (ed.). "Part Eight: Advancing Institutional Goals Through Enrollment Management." In A. Westley Rowland (gen. ed.), *Handbook of Institutional Advancement: A Practical Guide to College and University Relations, Fund Raising, Alumni Relations, Government Relations, Publications, and Executive Management for Continued Advancement.* (2nd ed.) San Francisco: Jossey-Bass, 1986. 54 pages.

This section addresses the issues surrounding enrollment rates that have a wide-ranging and powerful impact on higher education in the United States and discusses the strong leadership necessary to manage the dynamic forces facing both the independent and public sectors. The selected chapters cover the variety of functions involved in enrollment management and the administrative activities that accomplish its goals and objectives. The authors cover topics such as student information systems, financial aid, and volunteer constituencies as vital facets of the advancement process. (For a description of the *Handbook* in its entirety, see entry number 54.)

420 Mayhew, Lewis B. *Surviving the Eighties: Strategies and Procedures for Solving Fiscal and Enrollment Problems.* San Francisco: Jossey-Bass, 1979. 350 pages.

This book offers a realistic approach to college management in an era of rising costs and declining enrollments. The author outlines specific steps that a financially troubled institution can take to improve fiscal health and details appropriate responsibilities for faculty and administration in ensuring institutional vitality. He also discusses the development of new institutional clienteles and pitfalls to avoid in seeking new students and includes a checklist of 319 practical ideas for increasing income and cutting costs.

421 Miller, Bob W., Eddy, John P., and others. *Recruiting, Marketing and Retention in Institutions of Higher Education.* Lanham, Md.: University Press of America, 1983. 351 pages.

This work is a collection of twenty-two articles aimed at assisting institutions in implementing effective programs for marketing, recruitment, and retention. Topics include marketing concepts and strategies for higher education, techniques for effective communications, approaches to retention of minority students, and assessment of consultant needs for marketing and recruitment. The book includes a number of case studies from different types of institutions, an annotated bibliography, and several checklists.

422 Noel, Lee (ed.). *Reducing the Dropout Rate.* New Directions for Student Services, no. 3. San Francisco: Jossey-Bass, 1978. 108 pages.

This action-oriented resource guide is aimed at helping institutions reduce rates of attrition. It presents a wide range of concrete ideas, each linked to maintaining quality student services and academic programs, and contains an excellent annotated bibliography.

★**423** Noel, Lee, Levitz, Randi, and Saluri, Diana (eds.). *Increasing Student Retention: Effective Programs and Practices for Reducing the Dropout Rate.* San Francisco: Jossey-Bass, 1985. 450 pages.

The editors of this volume draw on the experiences of hundreds of institutions to offer practical advice and guidelines for improving retention and fostering student success. The book is divided into four parts: "Understanding Who Stays, Who Leaves, and What Makes the Difference," "Targeting Students at Risk for Dropping Out," "Fostering Retention Through Key Programs and Activities," and "Guidelines and Models for Achieving Retention Results." This study provides the advancement officer who works in enrollment management with valuable information as well as the experiences of many colleges and universities in dealing with the important problem of student retention.

424 Radner, Roy, and Miller, Leonard S. *Demand and Supply in U.S. Higher Education.* New York: McGraw-Hill, 1975. 468 pages.

Reporting on sophisticated statistical measurements of certain aspects of the supply of and demand for students, the authors detail college placement availability and faculty numbers needed. They construct illustrative models that demonstrate the application of their procedures to the econometric analysis of demand for freshman places and consider such factors as attendance costs, student and family incomes, student academic ability, and other traits.

425 Shulman, Carol H. *University Admissions: Dilemmas and Potentials.* ERIC/Higher Education Report no. 5. Washington, D.C.: American Association for Higher Education, 1977. 52 pages.

This publication provides an overall view of college admissions policy as it reflects social and marketing trends in the larger society. Topics include legal problems, college applicant pools, admissions policies and goals, and college admissions from the student's perspective.

426 Stark, Joan S. (ed.). *Promoting Consumer Protection for Students.* New Directions for Higher Education, no. 13. San Francisco: Jossey-Bass, 1976. 105 pages.

This book presents an effective discussion of the several factors that have created the consumer protection movement in higher education. It also examines the difficult and controversial issues surrounding the implementation of protective measures, emphasizing protection of students from misleading or inaccurate information and achieving a balance between institutional and student rights. The book's eight chapters present varying perspectives on the issue.

427 Upcraft, M. Lee (ed.). *Orienting Students to College.* New Directions for Student Services, no. 25. San Francisco: Jossey-Bass, 1984. 116 pages.

This guide details how to design a single comprehensive orientation program that will facilitate the adjustment of all students entering college—full and part time, residential and commuting, adults, veterans, minorities, transfers, and disabled persons. It examines the impact of college on the new student, presents orientation programs that can help students adjust, stay, and achieve, and offers practical information on all phases from planning to evaluation.

428 Williams, William G. *Enrollment Strategy.* Charlottesville, Va.: Share, 1981. 123 pages.

This useful manual contains 102 enrollment-growth suggestions, grouped under such headings as personnel policies, campus environment, and course announcements. The author's premise is that everyone at the institution must contribute to enrollment growth, and he offers a team approach to implementing his suggestions.

9

Management Resources for Advancement Officers and Executives

The success of any institutional advancement program depends largely on the effectiveness of its management. While an adequate budget, a well-trained and energetic staff, and a sympathetic administration are all important elements, no advancement program can succeed without capable top-level management. The executive manager must be concerned with planning, setting goals and objectives, establishing priorities, developing an organization, selecting, training, and motivating personnel, facilitating change, and evaluating results. This listing of duties in itself suggests the magnitude of the manager's responsibilities.

Most executives of institutional advancement programs are not trained managers. To a large extent, they have gone through the ranks of advancement departments, learning management on the job. Therefore, it is vitally important that continuing education, publications, institutes and workshops, and other programs be made available to managers in this area. Until recently, the formal organizations of institutional advancement officers have made few serious attempts to develop programs and activities of value to the executive manager. Happily, this is changing; the Council for Advancement and Support of Education has made this important area one of its major concerns for the years ahead.

One resource of potential value in developing managerial skills for advancement officers is the business community. While many of the techniques of business and corporate management can be usefully applied to management of institutional advancement,

176

there has been in the past a reluctance to adopt them. One source of this reluctance is a belief that the difference between the field of education and that of business is so great that it precludes any useful exchange of management models and skills. Certainly, there is a difference: colleges and universities exist not to make profit but to educate; they deal primarily with learning, with intangible ideas and concepts. Their "employees" are also different from those of business. But the manager in either situation must deal with budgets, with people, with goals and objectives, with evaluation, and with many other common elements, and there is much that the field of advancement can learn from the business world. The publications annotated in this chapter will help to bridge the gap between the professional managerial knowledge available to the business community and its application to higher education.

429 Adams, Carl R. (ed.). *Appraising Information Needs of Decision Makers.* New Directions for Institutional Research, no. 15. San Francisco: Jossey-Bass, 1977. 106 pages.

This is a collection of eight articles that provide specific suggestions for improving information-system development and implementation within higher education. Specific issues addressed include integrating resource allocation with academic planning, the uses of outcome data, and improving the quality of information-seeking questions.

★**430** Barnard, Chester I. *Functions of the Executive.* Cambridge, Mass.: Harvard University Press, 1960. 334 pages.

This book is still one of the most thought-provoking publications on organization and management. The book endures not only because it has been influential in the literature of organization but, more important, because it continues to offer insights into the field. The author's purpose is to provide a comprehensive theory of cooperative behavior in formal organizations. He points out that cooperation originates in people's need to accomplish purposes that they are unable to accomplish individually and that willingness to cooperate, the ability to communicate, and the existence and acceptance of purpose are essential to the survival of an organization.

431 Baron, Robert A. *Behavior in Organizations: Understanding and Managing the Human Side of Work.* Boston: Allyn & Bacon, 1983. 583 pages.

This textbook provides broad and up-to-date coverage of research in organizational behavior, including recent advances in related fields. Part 1 defines organizational behavior and examines research methods used in the field. Parts 2 and 3 examine the individual and group processes at work in organizational settings, and part 4 provides suggestions for enhancing organizational effectiveness. The book is written in an informal style and includes many reader aids (tables, word diagrams, chapter outlines, summaries, case studies, and so on).

432 Bittel, Lester R. *Leadership: The Key to Management Success.* New York: Franklin Watts, 1984. 201 pages.

The author of this book makes the point that knowledgeable managers must continually bridge the gap between the experiences of real-life situations and the proven results of wide-ranging research and management theories. He explains how effective leadership skills can improve one's interpersonal relationships on all levels, induce higher outputs and smoother employee operations, and help create a closer match between productivity and morale throughout the work environment. This work is a self-teaching guide that covers the basics and describes a variety of illustrative applications.

433 Blake, Robert R., and Mouton, Jane Srygley. *Solving Costly Organizational Conflicts: Achieving Intergroup Trust, Cooperation, and Teamwork.* San Francisco: Jossey-Bass, 1984. 327 pages.

This book offers a new approach to solving organizational conflicts. It examines the underlying causes of numerous conflict situations and presents clear guidelines for implementing the new approach in a variety of settings. The suggestions offered can help large and small organizations to resolve disputes and encourage integration among varying positions of group members.

434 Blake, Robert R., Mouton, Jane Srygley, and Williams, Martha Shipe. *The Academic Administrator Grid: A Guide to Developing Effective Management Teams.* San Francisco: Jossey-Bass, 1981. 423 pages.

This book applies Blake and Mouton's management grid to college and university administration. It offers readers a procedure for assessing assumptions about administration and leadership—including how they make decisions, resolve conflicts, express convictions, and exert effort—and shows how the Academic Administrator Grid distinguishes among administrators in terms of these assumptions. The authors identify five primary styles of leadership and describe how these differ in the planning, organizing, directing, controlling, and staffing of university operations. They present case examples of how different leaders handle key tasks, explain why team leadership is the most effective approach, and discuss how it can be fully implemented to ensure institutional excellence.

435 Bolman, Lee G., and Deal, Terrence E. *Modern Approaches to Understanding and Managing Organizations.* San Francisco: Jossey-Bass, 1984. 325 pages.

This book explains how current organizational research can be applied to solving particular problems and improving management practices. The authors describe and compare four approaches to organizational management (structural, human resource, political, and symbolic) and suggest techniques applicable to each. Using case studies and examples from businesses, nonprofit institutions, and colleges, this book illustrates the principles of modern organizational theory as they relate to formal and informal structure, motivation for increased productivity, and the transformation of conflict and power struggles into commitments of unity and purpose.

436 Council for Advancement and Support of Education. "Extending Your Resources Through Management." *CASE Currents,* 1975, *1* (entire issue 3).

This special issue of *CASE Currents* is devoted to the topic of effective management techniques and strategies. Articles cover such topics as planning as an art form, how to manage more by doing less, and how to develop program evaluations.

★**437** Council for Advancement and Support of Education. "Manage For Results." *CASE Currents,* 1978, *4* (entire issue 1).

In this special issue of *CASE Currents,* the emphasis is on planning through the use of management by objectives. Techniques, suggestions, and examples are given.

438 Council for Advancement and Support of Education. "Hiring and Firing." *CASE Currents,* 1981, *7* (entire issue 8).

This special issue of *CASE Currents* discusses various aspects of hiring and firing, including ten hiring do's and don't's, legal aspects of hiring, how to check references, how to fire, and what to do if you are fired. It describes qualifications to look for in a fund raiser, alumni administrator, news bureau director, periodical editor, publications director, and governmental relations director.

439 Council for Advancement and Support of Education. "Productivity: Part I." *CASE Currents,* 1983, *9* (entire issue 5).

In this first of a series of special issues devoted to productivity, *CASE Currents* presents a collection of eight articles that deal with such topics as supervising staff, teamwork, quality circles, motivating employees, and using students in public relations. The last article is a checklist for assessing the strengths and weaknesses of a fund-raising operation.

440 Council for Advancement and Support of Education. "Productivity Part II: Programs." *CASE Currents,* 1983, *9* (entire issue 6).

This issue, featuring some of the best *CASE Currents* articles, provides practical tips to help you manage your time, your work, and your staff more productively. Techniques examined include organizing work schedules, setting deadlines, delegating responsibilities, setting aside creative time for big projects, using idle time efficiently, and stopping procrastinating.

441 Council for Advancement and Support of Education. "Time Management." *CASE Currents,* 1983, *9* (9), 14–24.

This *CASE Currents* special insert features five articles on time management. Included are tips on making time for creativity in a crowded agenda, a description of how the development office of one institution created a two-hour quiet time for creativity, helpful hints for those who procrastinate, and general guidelines for gaining control over how you spend your time.

★442 Deegan, Arthur Y., II, and Fritz, Roger J. *MBO Goes to College.* Boulder: University of Colorado, 1975. 272 pages.

This practical workbook provides the reader with the basic concepts of management, tools for identifying and analyzing alternative styles of management, an understanding of the management by objectives (MBO) approach, and the skills necessary to apply MBO within higher education institutions. Each of the workbook's twelve sections contains an assortment of practical exercises. A supplementary reading list is also provided.

443 Drucker, Peter F. *Effective Executive.* New York: Harper & Row, 1967. 178 pages.

This is a systematic study of what effective executives do differently from others. The most important point, according to the author, is that effectiveness can be learned. He discusses the uses of time, the elements of decision making, and effective means for understanding executive problems and their resolutions.

444 Dunsing, Richard J. *You and I Have Simply Got to Stop Meeting This Way.* New York: American Management Association, 1979. 164 pages.

This book offers help to both leaders and participants in improving the quality of meetings. It discusses what is wrong with many meetings and the games that are played by participants and explains how to analyze meetings and diagnose their failings, with suggestions for creative ways to initiate change. Dunsing concludes that good meetings are those that have effectively mastered the following three dimensions: the processes of meeting management, the process of human interaction, and the physical setting. This is good reading for anyone who attends or chairs regular work meetings.

445 Eble, Kenneth E. *The Art of Administration: A Guide for Academic Administrators.* San Francisco: Jossey-Bass, 1978. 160 pages.

This book explores specific responsibilities and tasks of the academic administrator and offers practical assistance in a number of areas, including improvement of communications methods, motivating, encouraging, and effectively utilizing personnel, the pitfalls of divorcing long-range planning from day-to-day concerns of faculty and students, and ways of finding equilibrium among conflicting demands. Eble views administration as a professional "art" and discusses the development of individual qualities that are needed for success. He explains why the best administrators are those who act as keepers of the conscience as well as managers of affairs.

446 Etzioni, Amitai. *Complex Organizations.* New York: Free Press, 1961. 559 pages.

This book presents a threefold typology of organizations based on the means of power used to secure the compliance of subordinates: coercion (for example, prisons), remuneration (for example, factories), and manipulation of symbols (for example, churches). It includes thought-provoking discussion and examples.

447 Gardner, John. *Self Renewal: The Individual and the Innovative Society.* New York: Harper & Row, 1964. 141 pages.

This book addresses the need for creating conditions conducive to renewal—of self, organization, and society. Gardner begins with a discussion of the cycle of growth, decay, and renewal and then considers such topics as the obstacles to renewal, conditions of renewal, educating for renewal, the need for innovation and commitment, and organizing for renewal. He examines how our attitudes toward the future influence our ability for renewal and how continuous renewal of society must include the renewal of its values and beliefs as well.

448 Harvey, L. James. *Managing Colleges and Universities by Objectives.* Littleton, Colo.: Ireland Educational Corporation, 1976. 115 pages.

This book, written in a clear, concise fashion, provides the reader with the background and principles of MBO as it has been applied to institutions of higher education. It describes how to implement MBO, how to write objectives, and how to link MBO with management information systems, the planning, programming, and budgeting system, instruction by objectives, and various evaluation schemes. Appendixes include examples of one- and five-year plans from a community college, a four-year college, and a university. An MBO readiness inventory is also included.

449 Hopkins, David S. P., and Schroeder, Roger G. (eds.). *Applying Analytic Methods to Planning and Management.* New Directions for Institutional Research, no. 13. San Francisco: Jossey-Bass, 1977. 117 pages.

This volume is concerned with the practical use of operations research in institutions of higher education. The collection of six papers presents tried approaches to faculty resource planning, student enrollment forecasting, financial modeling, departmental faculty scheduling, cost analysis, and management-systems design.

450 Jacobson, Harvey K. (ed.). "Part One: Management Challenges and Strategies." In A. Westley Rowland (gen. ed.), *Handbook of Institutional Advancement: A Practical Guide to College and University Relations, Fund Raising, Alumni Relations, Government Relations, Publications, and Executive Management for Continued Advancement.* (2nd ed.) San Francisco: Jossey-Bass, 1986. 106 pages.

This section offers a series of thought-provoking discussions of management practices, speaking to the vital connections between management theories and current practices in institutional advancement. The authors discuss the nature of management, with emphasis on the differences between profit and nonprofit organizations. Especially valuable is a discussion of the qualities of successful managers. The chapters included cover organizational structure and leadership, interdisciplinary studies and their contributions to effecting social and institutional change, the management of planning, human resources, the use of volunteers, financial resources, and technological applications. The final chapter is of special interest to the advancement professional, as it deals with the tools for successful management—research and evaluation. (For a description of the *Handbook* in its entirety, see entry number 54.)

451 Kets De Vries, Manfred F. R., and Miller, Danny. *The Neurotic Organization: Diagnosing and Changing Counterproductive Styles of Management.* San Francisco: Jossey-Bass, 1984. 241 pages.

Using analogies from psychology, this book demonstrates how organizations, as well as people, can be neurotic. Drawing on their work as consultants, the authors detail five different types of organizational neuroses: paranoid, compulsive, dramatic, depressive, and schizoid. They show how each affects planning, decision making, organizational culture, and individuals and offer ways of diagnosing problems and promoting organizational and individual change.

★**452** Leslie, John W. *Focus on Understanding and Support.* Washington, D.C.: American College Public Relations Association, 1969. 129 pages.

This book is concerned solely with the management—planning, implementation, and evaluation—of programs and activities expressly designed to advance the understanding and support of institutions of higher education. The content is based on an extensive study that collected performance information from 1962 to 1968.

★**453** Leslie, John W. "A Resource Allocation Information System: For Managing an Institutional Advancement Program." *ACPRA College and University Journal*, 1973, *12* (3), 19–29.

This article describes a computerized resource-allocation information system that can enable institutions to assemble data for planning, controlling, and evaluating the institutional advancement function. The system described provides two basic worksheets: the institutional advancement program chart, a spreadsheet for recording expenditures by activity (such as information services, government relations, or fund solicitation), and a professional staff time sheet, categorized so that various advancement activities can be planned and accounted for accurately.

★**454** Lippitt, Gordon L., Langseth, Petter, and Mossop, Jack. *Implementing Organizational Change: A Practical Guide to Managing Change Efforts.* San Francisco: Jossey-Bass, 1985. 200 pages.

This authoritative book gives practical, step-by-step advice on how to analyze the changes needed within an organization—and how to implement those changes efficiently, effectively, and with the support of all involved. It discusses ways of determining exactly what kinds of changes are required to increase organizational effectiveness, solve problems, adapt to new conditions, and move in a positive direction. It also provides a variety of tables, graphs, and forms that can be used as models in implementing and evaluating organizational change.

455 Odiorne, George S. *Strategic Management of Human Resources: A Portfolio Approach.* San Francisco: Jossey-Bass, 1984. 356 pages.

Odiorne's approach to managing human resources in both public and private organizations views employees as assets and applies techniques designed to manage investment portfolios to the management of employees. The book is divided into four parts, which discuss the strategic approach and how portfolio analysis can be applied to human resource management; strategies for managing high-performing employees; managing poor performers; and implementing portfolio management strategies, with an example of a model program.

★456 Peters, Thomas J., and Waterman, Robert H., Jr. *In Search of Excellence.* New York: Warner Books, 1982. 360 pages.

This book focuses on eight characteristics found to be common to America's best-run companies: a bias for action; closeness to the customer; autonomy and entrepreneurship; productivity through people; hands-on value drives; "sticking to the knitting"; simple form–lean staff; and simultaneous loose-tight properties. Advancement officers can see how these characteristics of excellence relate to their own programs and organizations.

457 Radock, Michael (ed.). "Part Six: Executive Management." In A. Westley Rowland (gen. ed.), *Handbook of Institutional Advancement: A Practical Guide to College and University Relations, Fund Raising, Alumni Relations, Government Relations, Publications, and Executive Management for Continued Advancement.* (1st ed.) San Francisco: Jossey-Bass, 1977. 81 pages.

In the first edition of the *Handbook,* this section focuses on effective management as fundamental to the success of any institutional enterprise. Nine chapters cover all aspects of managing the advancement function, including the management of planning, goals, objectives, and priorities; personnel management; resource management; organization and structure; and the roles of evaluation and research. The authors state that successful management on the campus requires an understanding of the educational system and the values that motivate it, and they discuss the many and varied groups that today's educational administrator must deal with: government at all levels; unions and professional associations; faculty and staff; private donors, alumni, parents, and vendors; the governing board, which may be either publicly elected or politically appointed; and competitors in recruiting students and staff. (For a description of the *Handbook* in its entirety, see entry number 54.)

★**458** Rowland, A. Westley. "The Management of an Institutional Advancement Program." *College and University Journal*, 1974, *13*, 4–12.

Focusing on the role of the executive manager in institutional advancement, this article discusses ten areas of importance to the manager, including goals and priority setting, organization and personnel management, budgeting, and program development.

★**459** Schein, Edgar H. *Organizational Culture and Leadership: A Dynamic View*. San Francisco: Jossey-Bass, 1985. 358 pages.

The author carefully defines *organizational culture* to make it a truly useful concept for understanding and managing organizations. He draws on a wide range of managerial, psychological, and social research, as well as on his twenty-five years of consulting experience. He offers a penetrating analysis of culture in organizations and shows how organizational cultures begin, develop, and change in response to circumstances. Helpful to the advancement manager are the discussions of the role of the top executive in shaping and reinforcing culture; ways in which an organization's leaders can create, manage, and, if necessary, modify a particular organizational culture; and a rigorous method for uncovering and analyzing the beliefs and assumptions that form the basis of an organization's culture.

460 Scott, Robert A. (ed.). *Determining the Effectiveness of Campus Services.* New Directions for Institutional Research, no. 41. San Francisco: Jossey-Bass, 1984. 93 pages.

This sourcebook offers guidelines for assessing the quality, effectiveness, and efficiency of a number of campus services and activities, such as public relations, student services, academic libraries, and computing facilities, as well as alliances between industry and the university. It explains how to establish criteria for effective performance in each area on the basis of such institutional factors as size, goals, and available resources. It also offers methods for assessing institutional ineffectiveness and a strategy for organizational improvement. Suggestions for further reading are included.

461 Selznick, Philip. *Leadership in Administration.* New York: Harper & Row, 1957. 162 pages.

This seminal presentation defines and elaborates organizational leadership as "infusion of value" in institutional behaviors.

462 Shtogren, John A. (ed.). *Administrative Development in Higher Education: The State of the Art.* Vol. 1. Richmond, Va.: Dietz Press, 1978. 205 pages.

This volume is a collection of sixteen articles on the evaluation and development of college and university administrators, from department heads to college presidents. The articles provide candid insights on what is being attempted, what is working, and what is missing; they offer practical suggestions as well. Some of the articles deal with such general topics as creating a climate for administrative development in the context of community colleges and consortia, while others describe and analyze specific methods, such as the Chico Experiment and a pilot project by the H. E. Management Institute.

463 Smith, Virginia Carter, and Said, Carolyn (eds.). *How to Improve Your Productivity*. Washington, D.C.: Council for Advancement and Support of Education, 1984. 53 pages.

This collection of twenty-five of the best articles from *CASE Currents* offers practical tips on managing time more effectively. Selections describe how you can get ahead in the small shop, motivate yourself and your staff, and improve the effectiveness of alumni, publications, public relations, and fund-raising programs.

464 Sprunger, Benjamin E., and Bergquist, William H. *Handbook for College Administration*. Washington, D.C.: Council for the Advancement of Small Colleges, 1978. 340 pages.

This publication is the result of two years of program experimentation, research, and writing on college administration and management. It covers principles of college administration, planning, organizing, personnel selection, leadership, and evaluation.

465 Tannenbaum, Robert, Margulies, Newton, Massarik, Fred, and Associates. *Human Systems Development: New Perspectives on People and Organizations*. San Francisco: Jossey-Bass, 1985. 600 pages.

Twenty-three original chapters by leading authorities on management, organizational behavior, and organizational development present a comprehensive account of work being done on the leading edge of organizational theory and practice. This book offers new insights into the role of leadership in shaping organizational culture—and how culture affects leadership styles. It examines the roles that myths and rituals play in creating, maintaining, and guiding organizations, shows how conflict can present opportunities to leaders, and describes five conflict-handling strategies, with guides on when to use them. It also investigates the important role of values in managerial decision making. It concludes with an epilogue by Warren Bennis, "Understanding the Riddle of People and Organizations."

10

The Chief Executive and Advancement

The president of a college or university is the central figure in a successful advancement program—in reality, the institution's chief advancement officer. The president sets the parameters of what advancement can accomplish, is responsible for the climate in which its activities are carried out, and is (or should be) an active participant in many of those activities. He or she is the interface among all the constituencies of the institution and carries the greatest influence with them.

Because of this central role, there must be a special and close relationship between the president and the manager of institutional advancement. It is essential that the goals and objectives of the advancement program coincide with and be supportive of those of the institution. This can happen only when the president and the manager of advancement work together to make achievement possible. The president must work with the advancement staff to maximize communication with both internal and external audiences; in turn, the advancement manager must make careful use of the president's time, calling on the chief executive only for those situations where he or she can have the greatest impact on the institution's publics. The publications annotated in this chapter offer guidance in developing this very important relationship.

466 American Association of State Colleges and Universities. *Defining Leadership.* Washington, D.C.: American Association of State Colleges and Universities, 1980. 49 pages.

Based on four presentations made at the 1979 Summer Council of Presidents, this booklet addresses the broad questions surrounding what presidential leadership is and how it is exercised today. It examines possible presidential responses to a range of specific campus needs, such as strengthening general education, managing time, and balancing constituency conflicts.

467 Association of American Colleges. *The President's Role in Development.* Washington, D.C.: Association of American Colleges, 1975. 57 pages.

This work is a collection of presentations from three seminars on the president's role in the development of private support held in the mid 1970s. Among the issues treated are the president's management role in development and the president's leadership in motivating trustees, volunteers, and donors. The work emphasizes the need for long-range master plans and includes a bibliography.

468 Benezet, Louis T., Katz, Joseph, and Magnuson, Frances W. *Style and Substance: Leadership and the College Presidency.* Riverside, N.J.: Macmillan, 1981. 137 pages.

In this volume, administrators, faculty, students, and presidents express their thoughts on what it means to be a college president. Topics such as presidential background, management skills, and other aspects of the office are discussed.

469 Carbone, Robert F. *Presidential Passages.* Riverside, N.J.: Macmillan, 1981. 112 pages.

This collection of interviews with 1,460 former presidents offers candid, revealing, and often irreverent views of the presidential office and the decisions that led individuals to enter into and leave it.

470 Cohen, Michael D., and March, James G. *Leadership and Ambiguity.* New York: McGraw-Hill, 1973. 270 pages.

This book offers an interesting analysis of leadership in the face of uncertainties as exemplified by the ambiguous role of college president.

★471 Council for Advancement and Support of Education. "Working with Your President in PR." *CASE Currents,* 1980, *6* (9), 8–20.

This special insert examines the role of the president in public relations and discusses the ways in which presidents view public relations personnel. Four articles cover the rules for ensuring that public relations maintains a leading edge; the president's expectations of the public relations director; how and why many presidents view students as the "main image makers"; and how public relations professionals can better help presidents understand their positions and the field.

★472 Council for Advancement and Support of Education. "The President's Role in the Capital Campaign." *CASE Currents,* 1984, *10* (entire issue 1).

Many of the articles in this special issue of *CASE Currents* were written by presidents, who offer advice on what to do and what not to do, as well as information on what presidents like and dislike about fund raising. A discussion of how a strong partnership between president and vice-president can help fund raising highlights the case of the University of San Diego. Brend Brecher offers an insightful look at how a development officer should deal with a president who will not or cannot raise money.

473 Cowley, W. H. *Presidents, Professors, and Trustees: The Evolution of American Academic Government.* (Donald T. Williams, Jr., ed.) San Francisco: Jossey-Bass, 1980. 260 pages.

This book reviews the misconceptions about academic governance that have embittered the relations among faculty, students, administrators, and other participants in academic policy making. It summarizes the major positions that each of these groups have held about academic governance, explains the evolution of these views, and recommends ways to improve future decision making through better understanding.

★**474** Fisher, James L. (ed.). *Presidential Leadership in Advancement Activities.* New Directions for Institutional Advancement, no. 8. San Francisco: Jossey-Bass, 1980. 98 pages.

College and university presidents and advancement professionals describe ways in which presidents can take the lead in advancing the ideals and objectives of their institutions by improving government relations, public relations, and fund raising.

475 Kerr, Clark. *Presidents Make a Difference: Strengthening Leadership in Colleges and Universities.* Washington, D.C.: Association of Governing Boards of Universities and Colleges, 1984. 161 pages.

This highly acclaimed study shows trustees how to counteract the forces that can impair a president's ability to lead. It outlines the proper checks and balances needed to sustain campus leaders in their demanding jobs and makes numerous recommendations derived from a three-year study conducted by the author and the Association of Governing Boards' National Commission on Strengthening Presidential Leadership.

476 Smith, G. T. "Chapter Fifty-four: The Chief Executive and Advancement." In A. Westley Rowland (gen. ed.), *Handbook of Institutional Advancement: A Practical Guide to College and University Relations, Fund Raising, Alumni Relations, Government Relations, Publications, and Executive Management for Continued Advancement.* (2nd ed.) San Francisco: Jossey-Bass, 1986. 9 pages.

In this chapter of the *Handbook,* Smith states that successful institutional advancement depends ultimately on the chief

executive's willingness and capacity for leadership of the advancement effort. He contends that there are four essential tasks for the
chief executive: to clearly and convincingly articulate the mission
and values of the institution; to secure the sponsorship of the
governing board; to recruit and maintain a close relationship with
the chief advancement officer; and to serve the advancement
program actively and enthusiastically, with primary attention to
securing major gift support. (For a description of the *Handbook* in
its entirety, see entry number 54.)

477 Stohe, Harold W. *The American College President.* New
York: Fund for Advancement of Education, 1961. 180
pages.

Stohe, president of Queens College, provides a classic report on
some of the problems—as well as the pleasures—of being a college
president. This well-written book discusses such issues as relationships with the board, administrators, faculty, and students, the role
of the president in public relations and fund raising, the authority
of the president, and the uses of a philosophy of education. Stohe
draws on his own experience as well as the experiences of other
noteworthy college presidents.

478 Walker, Donald E. *The Effective Administrator: A Practical Approach to Problem Solving, Decision Making, and
Campus Leadership.* San Francisco: Jossey-Bass, 1979. 208
pages.

This book presents a theoretical perspective on administration and
numerous practical strategies for handling particular situations.
The author demonstrates how a realistic understanding of the
political nature of the campus community will promote effective
problem solving, recommends ways for dealing with day-to-day
problems resulting from budget reductions, declining enrollments,
and other adverse developments, and outlines successful methods
for implementing unpopular policies, negotiating difficult
decisions, reducing hostility, increasing participation of faculty,
students, and other parties, and responding to accusations and
criticism.

Two-Year Colleges

479 Alfred, Richard, Elsner, Paul, and LeCroy, Jan (eds.). *Emerging Roles for Community College Leaders.* New Directions for Community Colleges, no. 46. San Francisco: Jossey-Bass, 1984. 132 pages.

This sourcebook focuses on issues of change within the context of community college leadership. It discusses advancing technology, public policy initiatives by government agencies, demographics, economics, societal attitudes, and the development of reforms that can better prepare community colleges to meet the challenges that all colleges currently face.

480 Bender, Louis W., and Wygal, Benjamin R. (eds.). *Improving Relations with the Public.* New Directions for Community Colleges, no. 20. San Francisco: Jossey-Bass, 1977. 104 pages.

This volume provides comprehensive descriptions of external and media relations programs for two-year colleges. Topics include the components of a model public relations program, the methods involved in planning a community-based marketing program, the legal aspects of public relations, authority and control, and means for assessing results.

11

Advancing Two-Year Colleges, Independent Schools, and Small, Developing Institutions

Most of the material in this book has been directed at the typical four-year college or university. The publications annotated in this chapter address the needs of special types of institutions—the two-year colleges, independent schools, and small and developing institutions. Because of the differences between these and the four-year institutions—differences in history and tradition, scope of operation, methods of financing, the stage of their advancement activities, the nature of their leadership, and the clientele they serve—they have special needs in carrying out their advancement functions. While much of the literature discussed in the previous chapters has value for these institutions, techniques and procedures for such areas as fund raising, institutional relations, and publications may have to be adapted to their needs. Sometimes this may mean merely a reduction in scale; in other cases, one function of advancement may have to be stressed over another, or new and different techniques may have to be developed. The literature annotated here has been specifically selected to meet the particular needs of these special institutions.

196

★481 Bennett, John E. (ed.). *Building Voluntary Support for the Two-Year College.* New Directions for Community Colleges, no. 27. Washington, D.C.: Council for Advancement and Support of Education, 1979. 142 pages.

This handbook contains twenty-two chapters on fund raising, community relations, and alumni relations written specifically for the two-year college. It explains why two-year colleges need private funds and describes ways to establish a college foundation, do prospect research, write effective proposals, and conduct alumni telephone campaigns.

★482 Bryant, Peter S., and Johnson, Jane A. (eds.). *Advancing the Two-Year College.* New Directions for Institutional Advancement, no. 15. San Francisco: Jossey-Bass, 1982. 113 pages.

This comprehensive overview of opportunities and effective approaches for advancing community colleges recommends ways of establishing strong community relations, raising funds, cultivating alumni support, developing and coordinating a successful publications program, and strengthening marketing techniques.

483 Charles, Searle (ed.). *Balancing State and Local Control.* New Directions for Community Colleges, no. 23. San Francisco: Jossey-Bass, 1978. 108 pages.

This volume examines the successes and failures of various states in balancing local and state controls over community colleges. In so doing, it illuminates the issues and concerns raised by the encroachment of the state in policy formulation, decision making, and other prerogatives formerly held by local boards. The concluding chapter provides a useful overview of the literature on state and local positions.

484 Cohen, Arthur M., and Associates. *College Responses to Community Demands: The Community College in Changing Times.* San Francisco: Jossey-Bass, 1975. 190 pages.

The authors of this volume survey the entire spectrum of the internal and external forces that are reshaping the nature of the two-year college and evaluate the reactions of numerous college administrators to the implications of these forces for the future of community colleges. The book also contains a useful review of significant research and literature on this topic.

485 Cohen, Arthur M., and Brawer, Florence B. *The American Community College.* San Francisco: Jossey-Bass, 1982. 224 pages.

This book provides a comprehensive overview of community college education in the United States. Chapter 1 reviews the social forces that contributed to the development and expansion of community colleges. The changing patterns and characteristics of community college students are the focus of chapter 2, while chapter 3 examines issues related to faculty. Chapter 4 explores changes in college administration, and chapter 5 describes the various funding patterns used to finance community colleges. Instruction is considered in chapter 6, student services in chapter 7, and the positions of career, compensatory, and adult education in the community college curriculum in chapters 8, 9, and 10. Chapter 11 looks at the rise and fall of liberal arts, chapter 12 traces the development of general education curricula, and chapter 13 examines the social role of the community college. An annotated bibliography of major publications in the field is appended.

★**486** Council for Advancement and Support of Education. *Building Voluntary Support for the Two-Year College.* Washington, D.C.: Council for Advancement and Support of Education, 1979. 141 pages.

In this loose-leaf case-book on attracting voluntary support for community colleges, three major sections provide practical information on college fund raising, public relations, and alumni support. The book interweaves generalizations on the need for college fund raising, exhortations on the importance of voluntary support, and useful tips on how to perform the activity.

487 Harper, William A. *Community, Junior, and Technical Colleges.* Washington, D.C.: Hemisphere, 1977. 212 pages.

This work outlines and substantiates the contention that community support and cooperation are essential to the effectiveness of the community college. It discusses the uses of public relations and its important role of informing the community about the institution's mission and articulating the advantages that the community derives from supporting the institution.

488 Johnson, Jane A. "Chapter Fifty-five: Advancement Strategies for Two-Year Colleges." In A. Westley Rowland (gen. ed.), *Handbook of Institutional Advancement: A Practical Guide to College and University Relations, Fund Raising, Alumni Relations, Government Relations, Publications, and Executive Management for Continued Advancement.* (2nd ed.) San Francisco: Jossey-Bass, 1986. 16 pages.

This chapter brings together ideas of advancement professionals with experience in two-year institutions on how to cope in a changing environment with fiscal constraints, altered public attitudes, dramatic shifts in demographics, and the technology explosion. The author describes communication programs and techniques uniquely geared to building public support for the comprehensive community college. (For a description of the *Handbook* in its entirety, see entry number 54.)

489 Keim, William A., and Keim, Marybelle C. (eds.). *Marketing the Program*. New Directions for Community Colleges, no. 36. San Francisco: Jossey-Bass, 1981. 127 pages.

This volume discusses the use of marketing in community colleges, covering the four basic steps within the marketing arena: assessment, promotion, delivery, and evaluation. It offers practical and specific advice to the practitioner and provides questions and cautions to be considered by colleges engaged in marketing.

490 Luck, Michael F., and Tolle, Donald J. *Community College Development: Alternative Fund-Raising Strategies*. Indianapolis: Newkird, 1978.

Designed to provide data concerning the status of foundations and fund raising in public community colleges across the United States, this book offers specific information helpful in the establishment and operation of foundations and fund-raising programs. Though more than a "how-to" book, it does emphasize the pragmatic and useful.

491 Myran, Gunder A. (ed.). *Strategic Management in the Community College*. New Directions for Community Colleges, no. 44. San Francisco: Jossey-Bass, 1983. 121 pages.

This sourcebook emphasizes the viewpoint that community colleges need to move from operational to strategic management in the six primary areas of their operations: external relationships, internal communications and relationships, financial resource development and allocation, program development, staff development, and planning. It provides a comprehensive definition of strategic management and demonstrates means for its implementation through examples and discussion.

492 Sharron, Harvey W., Jr. (ed.). *The Community College Foundation*. Washington, D.C.: National Council for Resource Development, 1982. 321 pages.

This book presents a comprehensive description of the conceptualization and operations of the two-year college foundation. It provides college administrators and lay board members with the tools necessary to develop and organize such a foundation. Five major parts discuss the rationale, the national perspective, the president's perspective, administrative and management techniques, and strategies and techniques. Viewpoints of seventeen community college leaders shed light on the many different aspects of community college foundations and how they relate to business and the private sector.

493 Slabaugh, Darrell E. "Serving Diverse Alumni." *CASE Currents*, 1979, 5 (2), 22.

Using Kirkwood Community College as an example, the author treats the topic of working with the alumni of a community college. He suggests three questions for evaluating how well an institution is serving the alumni: How much money do we raise? What political impact do we have? How do we benefit Kirkwood? He discusses such activities developed by this community college as trips, reunions, legislative activities, special activities, fund raising, and record keeping.

★**494** Trent, Richard L. (ed.). *Public Relations in the Community College*. Washington, D.C.: Council for Advancement and Support of Education, 1981. 64 pages.

This work describes the basic principles of public and community relations, including public relations support services, alumni relations, photography and visual communications, printing and distribution, and the management of public relations operations.

495 Vaughan, George B., and Associates. *Issues for Community College Leaders in a New Era.* San Francisco: Jossey-Bass, 1983. 275 pages.

This book shows how community colleges can improve governance, curriculum, and student services in order to better meet current and future demands. Section 1 describes ways in which the college can serve increasing numbers of diverse students, including disadvantaged persons, the adult learner, and others with a wide range of skills and abilities. The special functions of the community college are addressed in section 2, which includes suggestions on providing remedial education and strengthening the transfer program. Issues concerning reformulating general education programs and redirecting student services are also addressed. The last section is concerned with managing the community college and includes examinations of leadership, alliances with business and industry, and the building of community support.

496 Woodress, Fred A. *Public Relations for Community/Junior Colleges.* Danville, Ill.: Interests, 1976. 62 pages.

In this useful sourcebook, Woodress, a veteran in the field, discusses the need for good public relations programs and outlines specific procedures for community and junior colleges.

Independent Schools

497 Gilbert, Edes P. "Chapter Fifty-six: Fostering Support for Independent Schools." In A. Westley Rowland (gen. ed.), *Handbook of Institutional Advancement: A Practical Guide to College and University Relations, Fund Raising, Alumni Relations, Government Relations, Publications, and Executive Management for Continued Advancement.* (2nd ed.) San Francisco: Jossey-Bass, 1986. 8 pages.

Following a short historical and philosophical treatment of the independent school and its role in this country, the author discusses special problems in securing support and understanding for these schools. Her major thesis is that the case for advancement in independent schools rests on the statement of mission for independent education, and she stresses increased endowments as one of their pressing needs. She concludes that independent schools must make a greater effort to get their fair share of support. (For a description of the *Handbook* in its entirety, see entry number 54.)

★**498** Whelan, Donald J. (ed.). *Handbook for Development Officers at Independent Schools.* (2nd ed.) Washington, D.C.: Council for Advancement and Support of Education, 1982. 350 pages.

This comprehensive guide to the principles and procedures of raising money for independent schools explains how to organize, build a staff, plan, recruit volunteers, use consultants, and evaluate the program. It outlines the fundamentals of capital campaigns, annual giving, and planned giving and offers suggestions for approaching foundations. It includes sections on fund raising, alumni programs, communications, constituency relations, and management.

Small and Developing Institutions

499 Carnegie Council on Policy Studies in Higher Education. *The States and Private Higher Education: A Proud Past and a Vital Future.* San Francisco: Jossey-Bass, 1977. 206 pages.

This report evaluates the impact of existing government programs on enrollments, finances, autonomy, and other conditions and offers recommendations for future action, with a focus on the state's responsibility for undergraduate education at nonprofit private institutions. It generally favors improvement of federal and state student aid policies as the major approach to public support for private higher education.

★**500** Council for Advancement and Support of Education. "The Small Shop." *CASE Currents,* 1981, 7 (entire issue 5).

In this special issue of *CASE Currents,* twelve authors from small-staff public relations operations cover such topics as staging a successful capital campaign, running a parents' program, using faculty to attract grant funds, and planning special events to garner media coverage. A round-up section gives hour- and dollar-stretching ideas from fifteen institutions.

501 Council for Advancement and Support of Education. "Fantastic Feats of Fund Raising: Small College Success Stories." *CASE Currents,* 1983, 9 (7), 16-27.

In this *CASE Currents* special insert, four small colleges describe their fund-raising successes. Their stories illustrate diverse ways of fund raising, from phonathons to deferred-giving programs, including a description of how one school raised more than half a million dollars in six weeks.

502 Falender, Andrew J., and Merson, John C. (eds.). *Management Techniques for Small and Specialized Institutions.* New Directions for Higher Education, no. 42. San Francisco: Jossey-Bass, 1983. 100 pages.

This collection of eleven articles focuses on the effective management of small institutions, analyzing an assortment of problems that the president and other senior administrators often face. The book provides detailed strategies for efficient functioning and financial planning, fund raising, student recruitment and admissions, public relations, organization and staffing of a small college, and use of outside resources.

★**503** Hunt, Susan (ed.), and Moore, R. Keith (comp.). *How to Make Big Improvements in the Small PR Shop.* Washington, D.C.: Council for Advancement and Support of Education, 1985. 116 pages.

This publication is directed at helping people in small shops who have one big problem—too much to do and too little to do it with.

It is filled with examples of what advancement professionals are doing on small campuses. The book covers methods that work, how to organize, objectives and priorities, establishing control through policies and guidelines, the routine jobs, transmitting information, and forms of internal organization. Advancement professionals in small shops will find this an indispensable publication.

504 West, Christopher. *Marketing on a Small Budget.* London: Associated Business Programmes, 1975. 210 pages.

This practical book shows how small organizations with limited funds can take advantage of modern marketing theory and practices. Chapters cover planning, research and development, test marketing, public relations, and organizing methods. The book also contains a number of checklists to assist readers in applying this information to their own institutions.

★**505** Willmer, Wesley K. (ed.). *Advancing the Small College.* New Directions for Institutional Advancement, no. 13. San Francisco: Jossey-Bass, 1981. 119 pages.

Focusing on the small college, this book discusses the variety of factors that are essential to successful advancement efforts. Among those emphasized are dynamic leadership, clarity of institutional mission and goals, use of simple marketing techniques, and effective use of consultants.

★**506** Willmer, Wesley K. *The Small College Advancement Program: Managing for Results.* Washington, D.C.: Council for Advancement and Support of Education, 1981. 145 pages.

Based on a study of 141 small institutions, this book examines institutional programs at small independent colleges. Particular attention is given to budget strategies, staff sizes, specific advancement activities, evaluation criteria, and suggestions for improvement at all program levels.

507 Willmer, Wesley K. "Chapter Fifty-seven: Advancing Small and Developing Institutions." In A. Westley Rowland (gen. ed.), *Handbook of Institutional Advancement: A Practical Guide to College and University Relations, Fund Raising, Alumni Relations, Government Relations, Publications, and Executive Management for Continued Advancement.* (2nd ed.) San Francisco: Jossey-Bass, 1986. 12 pages.

The author of this chapter contends that, while small and developing colleges are obviously more fragile and vulnerable to change than large institutions, they also tend to be more responsive, creative, and resilient. He argues that the challenge facing advancement officers at small institutions lies in these differences and presents a threefold focus for the advancement officer at a small college: cultivating friends, raising adequate funds, and attracting quality freshmen. (For a description of the *Handbook* in its entirety, see entry number 54.)

12

Legal Aspects
of Advancement

As society becomes more litigious, advancement practitioners must become increasingly aware of the legal implications of their work. One example of the importance of this awareness is seen in constitutional law. As shown by recent court interpretations of the First Amendment, guaranteeing freedom of association and expression, three apparent rights—the right of the public to know, the right of an institution to do its business, and the right of an individual to privacy—seem to be in inherent conflict, posing a substantial difficulty to the advancement officer. The problem is further aggravated by differences in the applicability of these rights within the public and private sectors.

In statutory law, some issues affect how advancement officers do their work, while others affect what they do. Changes in the copyright laws governing the extent to which material produced by one person may be used by another affect how advancement activities are carried out, as do laws of defamation (libel and slander) regarding injury to a person's reputation by publication of false and damaging information. Other new legal realities affect *what* the advancement professional does. Federal tax laws have important implications for the entire area of educational fund raising, especially regarding deferred giving and estate planning. In the areas of criminal and civil law, the institutional advancement practitioner needs to understand the legal implications of media relations. The publications annotated in this chapter are directed at assisting advancement professionals in understanding the legal aspects of what they do and how their work is carried out.

★**508** Baggerstock, Charles T. *Educational Fund-Raising and the Law*. Washington, D.C.: Council for Advancement and Support of Education, 1984. 81 pages.

This handbook on the law of educational fund raising can serve as a reference for practitioners or institutional legal counsel. It provides a brief historical look at educational fund raising in its legal context and discusses the law as it relates to the donor and the institution, covering charitable trusts, bequests, gifts, subscriptions, gifts in anticipation of death, and delayed or indefinite vesting of title to property. It also discusses how to enhance fund raising in the legal context, improve public image, influence legislation, and utilize the courts system. This book is especially valuable for those working in the areas of deferred giving and estate planning. It includes an excellent bibliography of legal reference works, books, articles, and dissertations and a complete glossary of legal terms.

509 Bedno, Jane H. "The Right to (Re) Print." *CASE Currents*, 1985, *11* (9), 17–21.

The author discusses the hazards involved in copyright, trademark, libel, privacy, and contract laws, with emphasis on the important areas of authorship, ownership, honor, and privacy. Of special value to advancement professionals are a discussion of rules for news releases, transfer of rights, and other forms of agreement and several helpful guides that furnish editors and writers with specific information concerning copyright.

510 Bickel, Robert D., and others (eds.). *The College Administrator and the Courts*. Asheville, N.C.: College Administration Publications, 1985. 346 pages.

This basic casebook, updated quarterly, covers higher court decisions affecting college administration and related cases of major importance (for coverage of decisions involving students, see entry number 523). Written in lay terms, it includes digests of illustrative examples. This work is a comprehensive reference, with cumulative cross indexes.

511 Cleveland, Harlan. *The Costs and Benefits of Openness.* Washington, D.C.: Association of Governing Boards of Universities and Colleges, 1985. 58 pages.

This book examines the advantages and drawbacks of state "sunshine" legislation, especially regarding disclosures about the selection and performance evaluations of college presidents, and analyzes how state open-meeting laws have affected candid deliberations at board meetings. The study and its conclusions are based upon extensive interviews and research of state ordinances, as well as discussions with media executives, college and state officials, and trustees. The work includes a state-by-state analysis of the laws regarding openness.

512 Hale, F. Dennis. "Libel Law and You." *CASE Currents,* 1985, *11* (9), 11–14.

This article is an important guide to avoiding libel suits for institutional editors. Pointing out that the best protection from libel suits is printing only the truth, the author responds to specific questions about libel, such as what libel is, who may be sued, what elements must be present in a libel suit, how publication is defined, and who is considered a public official or public figure. This is an excellent and up-to-date article on a topic of importance to publications specialists, periodical editors, and newswriters.

513 Hobbs, Walter C. (ed.). *Government Regulation of Higher Education.* Cambridge, Mass.: Ballinger, 1978. 117 pages.

This collection of essays argues the merits and demerits of government regulation for institutions of higher education and their personnel.

★514 Hobbs, Walter C. (ed.). *Understanding Academic Law.* New Directions for Institutional Advancement, no. 16. San Francisco: Jossey-Bass, 1982. 94 pages.

This book examines basic legal terms and principles relevant to institutional advancement in higher education. It clarifies the rights and responsibilities of advancement officers in the areas of fund raising, publications, maintenance and use of facilities, public relations, and campus speakers, with an emphasis on strengthening the institution's position regarding charges of legal improprieties.

515 Hobbs, Walter C. "Chapter Fifty-eight: Legal Issues in Institutional Advancement." In A. Westley Rowland (gen. ed.), *Handbook of Institutional Advancement: A Practical Guide to College and University Relations, Fund Raising, Alumni Relations, Government Relations, Publications, and Executive Management for Continued Advancement.* (2nd ed.) San Francisco: Jossey-Bass, 1986. 20 pages.

This chapter discusses several legal principles that bear upon the advancement function: First Amendment guarantees of freedom of association and expression, defamation, invasion of privacy, copyright, federal tax law, and criminal and civil ("tort") law. The author concludes that the law should be considered a boon to the realization of the advancement officer's purpose, not a disruption to be avoided. (For a description of the *Handbook* in its entirety, see entry number 54.)

516 Hopkins, Bruce R. *The Law of Tax-Exempt Organizations.* (7th ed.) New York: Ronald Press, 1986. 653 pages.

Updated annually, this classic reference remains the single most authoritative source of information on federal laws governing income-tax exemption and related rules for qualified organizations. Balancing factual coverage with lucid commentary and interpretation, it cites and explains all relevant cases, regulations, and rulings.

517 Kaplin, William A. *The Law of Higher Education: Legal Implications of Administrative Decision Making.* San Francisco: Jossey-Bass, 1978. 500 pages.

This work is a comprehensive sourcebook on law for administrators in higher education and their legal counsel. It provides detailed discussion of cases and cites and summarizes the laws, regulations, and court decisions pertaining to higher education. For each of the issues addressed, Kaplin clarifies the basic legal principles, analyzes the law's impact on institutional functions, points to future trends, and advises administrators on how to handle the issue in a way that is both legally sound and in the best interests of the institution. The book won the American Council on Education's 1978 book award.

518 Kaplin, William A. *The Law of Higher Education 1980.* San Francisco: Jossey-Bass, 1980. 184 pages.

Written to be used either independently or as a companion to *The Law of Higher Education* (see entry number 517), this book reviews the significant changes in laws affecting higher education from mid 1978 to 1980. It summarizes court decisions and agency regulations, analyzes implications, and indicates the educationally and legally sound response. Some of the topics covered are affirmative action in employment and admissions, faculty collective bargaining, age discrimination, discrimination against handicapped persons, and termination of tenured faculty's employment.

★519 Kaplin, William A. *The Law of Higher Education: A Comprehensive Guide to Legal Implications of Administrative Decision Making.* (2nd ed.) San Francisco: Jossey-Bass, 1985. 621 pages.

This revised and updated edition of the award-winning *Law of Higher Education* (see entry number 517) covers the broad range of legal issues, regulations, statues, and court decisions that affect postsecondary education. It integrates all material from the first edition and the 1980 supplementary volume (see entry number 518), with more than 50 percent new material covering the most current information on new legal developments that have taken place since 1980, including court authority to award conditional tenure as a remedy for sex discrimination, confidentiality of votes on tenure, sex discrimination in student admissions, campus security and violent crime on campus, institutions' liability for injuries due to student drinking, employment discrimination, sexual harassment, civil rights requirements for institutions that receive federal funds, and use of campus facilities by student religious groups. This is an excellent source for advancement practitioners who wish a broad treatment of legal issues affecting colleges and universities.

520 Meyers, John Holt. *Complying with IRS Regulations on Association Income.* Washington, D.C.: Council for Advancement and Support of Education, 1978. 14 pages.

This booklet, a detailed outline prepared for a CASE special conference, provides information about tax laws and IRS positions on such alumni programs as travel, insurance, and merchandising, as well as precautionary hints for avoiding unexpected tax problems. This publication is of special value to alumni administrators who sponsor auxiliary enterprises as part of the alumni relations program.

521 Taylor, Alton L. (ed.). *Protecting Individual Rights to Privacy in Higher Education.* New Directions for Institutional Research, no. 14. San Francisco: Jossey-Bass, 1977. 82 pages.

This study provides a general explanation of individual rights to privacy, identifies potential threats to and abuses of privacy rights, describes legal protections and technological safeguards, and gives direction to administrators who are responsible for protecting individual records. This helpful guide speaks to the rights of both students and staff.

522 Young, D. Parker (ed.). *Yearbook of Higher Education Law.* Topeka, Kans.: National Organization on Legal Problems of Education, 1985.

This comprehensive yearbook summarizes and analyzes all state and federal court cases involving higher education. Its index and table of contents are detailed, making it an easy-to-use reference.

523 Young, D. Parker, and others (eds.). *The College Student and the Courts*. Asheville, N.C.: College Administration Publications, 1985. 652 pages.

This basic casebook, written in lay language, covers higher court decisions affecting the relationships between the students and the institution, as well as the accompanying regulations and guidelines (for coverage of cases involving college administrators, see entry number 510). It provides comprehensive coverage of trend-setting and landmark decisions and digests of other cases that serve as illustrative examples. It is updated quarterly, with yearly cumulative cross indexes.

13

Keeping Abreast
of a Changing Field

The Need for Further Research

The need for colleges and universities for a wide variety of resources requires quantifiable research, but research in many of the functional program areas of advancement has been limited. Some practitioners feel that they are simply too busy doing their job to have time for evaluation and research. Others claim lack of expertise at doing research themselves or insufficient funds to employ outside consultants. Whatever the reasons given, they are no longer valid in a time when higher education needs maximum support and understanding from all its constituencies. Several institutions, including the State University of New York at Buffalo and the University of Michigan, have carried out self-studies. While this is probably the least objective method of research, such studies can form the basis for more formal evaluation, through review by outside professionals. The Council for Advancement and Support of Education (CASE) makes review teams available for this purpose.

One important area of research is the perceptions of the institutions held by its various publics—prospective and current students, their parents and high school counselors, alumni, faculty and staff, and such community interest groups as voters, business, clergy, government, and labor. The impact of a college or university on the community where it is located can be researched

Note: The author wishes to thank CASE vice-president Virginia Carter Smith and CASE staff members for suggestions concerning the future of advancement.

through a study of such factors as the effects on the community of campus visitors, building construction, and research projects, employment opportunities offered by the institution, student expenditures in the community, and continuing and adult education and other cultural and intellectual contributions. Insights into public attitudes toward higher education can be gained through a continuing study, such as has been carried out in Alabama, of voters' perceptions of their state's colleges and universities.

Alumni, one of an institution's most important publics, should be surveyed on an ongoing basis. Questions to be considered include how the alumni evaluate the education they received, whether they will enroll their children in the institution, whether they visit the campus often, and whether they engage in support activities, such as recruiting students, contributing to the alumni fund, and lobbying government.

In government relations (an increasingly important area of advancement), practitioners should be researching such issues as the factors that affect legislative decisions regarding education, the sources of legislators' attitudes toward a particular institution, the extent to which government is encroaching on college and university autonomy, and the major bases of federal policy on higher education in the United States. To determine the effectiveness of their program, advancement officers should consider such questions as the following: Are the techniques and relationships developed by government relations staff effective with federal, state, and local legislators? How effective is the lobbying program of the institution? What is the president's role in successful government relations?

Many questions need to be answered in the field of educational fund raising. Who gives to colleges and universities? What motivates them to give? What is the best yardstick for measuring fund-raising effectiveness? What are the best methods for securing big gifts? What institutional resources should be committed to fund raising? What percentage of money raised should go to cover costs? What undergraduate experiences tend to favor financial support by alumni (what is their "donor propensity")? To what extent should the president of a college or university be involved in fund raising? How should the professional fund-raising staff, trustees, faculty, staff, students, alumni, senior administrators, and friends be involved in fund raising? What background, education, and experiences produce the most effective fund raisers? What is the relationship of ecology to fund raising? What type of fund raising has the best chance for success in the future?

The area of publications and periodicals particularly lends itself to research and evaluation. To assess the effectiveness of an institution's publications with their various publics, the practitioner should determine how readable they are, how widely they are read, how favorable are the responses they produce, and how faithfully they mirror the true nature of the institution. Media relations is also an area requiring research. Advancement practitioners should continually monitor how their news releases are being received and used by newspapers, radio, television, and magazines. Investigation can determine whether written and film materials are produced in the right form and made available at the right time to encourage maximum use by the media and whether a proper balance is being maintained between electronic and print media.

Another area of investigation is how the advancement function can be organized for maximum effectiveness. Does it make any difference whether certain areas of advancement are organized as integral departments of a college or university or as separate and independent entities (as are alumni and fund-raising activities at some institutions)? Is a centralized or a decentralized structure more effective? How can the staff be evaluated? What is the most effective distribution of resources among the various advancement functions? Where can new staff be secured? What characteristics make for an effective advancement manager?

These are just some among the many important research questions that need to be explored by practitioners of institutional advancement.

Additional Resources

The most important association for advancement professionals is the Council for Advancement and Support of Education

(CASE) (see Chapter One for a discussion of CASE's history and some of its current activities). If there is only one publication that the advancement staff can read, it should be the journal of this organization, *Currents* (see Appendix B for a description of this journal). CASE also publishes a membership directory, a higher education directory, a placement letter, art packages, and other printed material; many of its publications are available on microfiche. Some of these publications are annotated in this book; a complete catalogue is provided in *CASE Resources*. This catalogue, as well as the publications themselves, can be obtained from CASE Publications Order Department, P.O. Box 298, Alexandria, Virginia 22313.

Another organization of interest to advancement practitioners is the Public Relations Society of America (PRSA), an individual-membership professional society of more than 12,000 members. Although it covers the whole range of public relations activities, PRSA does have an educational division. Its major services include programs for professional development and accreditation, an information center, and publications. Of special interest is a bibliography, published annually, with listings in four categories: general books; special-interest publications, in such areas as business and corporate management, ethics, publicity, communication, education, and law; bibliographies and directories; and periodicals. PRSA's official publication, the *Public Relations Journal*, is described in Appendix B.

In addition to the works annotated in this book, several bibliographies are useful to advancement practitioners. Scott M. Cutlip's *A Public Relations Bibliography* (2nd ed.; Madison: University of Wisconsin Press, 1965) covers sources of information on the theory, development, and practice of public relations; communication tools and media; and relations with external publics. Cletis Pride (ed.), *Securing Support for Higher Education: A Bibliographical Handbook* (New York: Praeger, 1972), published in cooperation with the American College Public Relations Association, covers books, periodicals, and other materials, with a "key-word-in-context" (KWIC) index. In *A Bibliographic Handbook* (vol. 2; Washington, D.C.: National Institute of Education, 1981), James L. Fisher, former president of CASE, does an excellent job of annotating major bibliographical contributions to advancement, covering advancement programs, public relations, fund raising, alumni relations, government relations, and communications.

Advancement practitioners who work with foundations and corporations should be acquainted with the Foundation Center, 79 Fifth Avenue, New York, N.Y. 10003. For twenty-eight years, the Foundation Center has been the national nonprofit clearinghouse for information on private philanthropy. The center can help grant seekers to meet their particular needs as they select from the more than 22,000 active U.S. foundations. It assists in matching foundation interests with nonprofit needs by publishing reference books on grant makers and disseminating information on grants and other issues of interest to nonprofit organizations through a nationwide public information and education program. Many of the publications of the center are annotated in this book; a complete catalogue is available from the center on request, as is a list of its more than 100 member institutions where its publications can be consulted.

The Future of Institutional Advancement

There is little question that advancement has established itself as an indispensable function in higher education. At most colleges and universities, it is recognized as one of the four essential programs, along with academics, finances, and student affairs. It is the opinion of this author that advancement programs will continue to grow and to make significant contributions to the support and understanding of higher education. The remainder of this chapter will describe some of the major concerns for the advancement professional and speculate on future trends in the field.

Advancement as a Profession. There is presently great interest in the development of advancement as a profession and its members as professionals. CASE has made this a high priority at both its national and district levels and is urging practitioners to advance their formal education by pursuing graduate degrees. The organization is developing a program, "Benchmarks of Professional Development," to provide members with a series of conferences, readings, and special projects in this area. There is also a need for a set of formal standards for admission to the advancement field, perhaps even some form of accreditation, so that advancement programs will be able to recruit the ablest and brightest young people into the field, retain those who join it, and provide more sophisticated programming for senior professionals. Research and evaluation, key hallmarks of a profession, will receive more attention from advancement professionals and CASE, leading to an even more extensive literature base for the field.

Every profession has a code of ethics and a means to enforce it. In 1982, after a year of deliberation of national and district leaders and volunteers, CASE adopted the first statement of ethics for the advancement field. This statement is intended to guide and reinforce ethical conduct throughout institutional advancement and to stimulate discussion of ethical issues that arise in the work of CASE professionals (see Appendix A for the full text of the statement). Each of the professional fields within CASE will develop its own particular statement of ethics, as well as case studies concerning ethical issues. Ethics will continue to be a topic for national and district CASE conferences.

Government Relations. There is no question that institutional advancement officers will have to become more concerned and involved with government at every level. The demands for responsibility, as well as the need for additional resources from the state and federal governments in particular, will require a more vigorous program of government relations.

The Role of Institutional Advancement. Advancement practitioners must continue to define their role in higher education and demonstrate more precisely how the goals and objectives of advancement mesh with those of the institution in general. This requires more than simply a definition of what advancement activities are; the profession must be concerned with developing a theory as well as a practical, how-to-do-it basis for the advancement function.

The New Technology. Advancement practitioners need increasingly to be informed about, use, and understand the new, ever-changing technology as it applies to the advancement field.

The information revolution is irreversible, and advancement professionals will have to be part of it. Already, many colleges are using computers and word processors in their work; the use of electronic mail, video cassette recorders, cable television, interactive communication, electronic data banks, processing networks, telecommunications, satellite broadcasting, video discs, laser printers, and similar technologies will lead to a reorganization of the ways advancement professionals communicate with people.

Alumni Relations. Alumni relations professionals will become increasingly concerned with younger alumni—those who have been out of college from one to ten years—and will develop special programs to build the base for a lifelong involvement with their institutions. Technology will be used to bring campus events and special classes to alumni throughout the world, in homes, in hotels and other meeting places, and at alumni club meetings. Continuing education for alumni will grow and expand, both on and off the campus, even reaching those in remote areas through the new technology. Expanded alumni programs for undergraduate students will help them to understand the role and functions of alumni while they are still on campus. Professionalism will increase among chief alumni officers, and more people will make alumni work a life career.

These, then, are some of the concerns, predictions, and hopes for the future of the advancement field. Together, they represent a challenge for the year 2000 and beyond.

Appendix A

CASE Statement of Ethics for Advancement Professionals

Institutional advancement professionals, by virtue of their special responsibilities within the academic community, represent their colleges, universities, and schools to the larger society. They have, therefore, a special duty to exemplify the best qualities of their institutions, and to observe the highest standards of personal and professional conduct.

In so doing, they promote the merits of their institutions, and of education generally, without disparaging other colleges and schools;

Their words and actions embody respect for truth, fairness, free inquiry, and the opinions of others;

They respect all individuals without regard to race, color, sex, creed, ethnic or national identity, handicap, or age;

They uphold the professional reputation of other advancement officers, and give credit for ideas, words, or images originated by others;

They safeguard privacy rights and confidential information;

They do not grant or accept favors for personal gain, nor do they solicit or accept favors for their institutions where a higher public interest would be violated;

They avoid actual or apparent conflicts of interest and, if in doubt, seek guidance from appropriate authorities;

They follow the letter and spirit of laws and regulations affecting institutional advancement;

They observe these standards and others that apply to their professions, and actively encourage colleagues to join them in supporting the highest standards of conduct.

Appendix B

Periodicals, Newsletters, and Journals for Advancement Professionals

AACJC Letter. Washington, D.C.: American Association of Community and Junior Colleges. Published weekly. The only national weekly newsletter exclusively for community, technical, and junior college leaders, this publication includes timely, topical briefs on cost-effective management, marketing and advancement opportunities, current legislative concerns and federal policies, and the latest statistical data.

AAHE Bulletin. Washington, D.C.: American Association for Higher Education. Published monthly (except June and July). This sixteen-page publication features commentary and debate, summaries of research reports on innovative programs, and briefs on association activities.

Administrative Science Quarterly. Ithaca, N.Y.: Johnson Graduate School of Management, Cornell University. Published quarterly. Dedicated to advancing the understanding of administration through empirical investigation and theoretical analysis, this publication presents articles on organizational behavior from both a macro- and a micro-analytical perspective. It is indexed annually in the December issue.

Administrator: The Management Newsletter for Higher Education. Madison, Wis.: Magna Publications. Published bimonthly. This newsletter provides ongoing information about the activities of colleges and universities around the country. It presents a variety of short notices that review current problems, highlight creative solutions, and summarize recent court cases affecting higher education.

Advancement Newsletter. Washington, D.C.: Office for the Advancement of Public Negro Colleges (OAPNC), National Association of State Universities and Land-Grant Colleges. Published periodically. This newsletter informs the news media, foundations, public and private agencies, corporations, and OAPNC member institutions on the work of historically black public colleges, particularly in the area of development.

Advisor. Annandale, Va.: Association of Community College Trustees. 10 issues annually. This newsletter contains federal news, association news, and a variety of topics of interest to community college trustees.

AGB Reports: The Journal of the Association of Governing Boards of Universities and Colleges. Washington, D.C.: Association of Governing Boards of Universities and Colleges. Published bimonthly. This journal and its companion monthly newsletter, *AGB Notes,* are devoted to trusteeship and the issues that affect board members and their institutions. Articles discuss trends, problems, and new ideas that are aimed at increasing the effectiveness of boards and trustees.

ASHE-ERIC Higher Education Research Report Series. Washington, D.C.: Educational Resources Information Center, Association for the Study of Higher Education. 10 reports annually. This is an annual series of ten literature-review monographs. Each report analyzes a specific problem in higher education on the basis of a thorough research of pertinent literature and institutional experiences. Topic areas identified by a national survey are discussed by noted practitioners and scholars, and manuscripts are reviewed by area experts prior to publication.

Business Officer. Washington, D.C.: National Association of College and University Business Officers. Published monthly. This publication provides the campus administrator with monthly reports on national events that can have an effect on higher education. Developments in federal government and financial areas dominate coverage. It is indexed annually in the August issue.

Change: The Magazine of Higher Learning. Washington, D.C.: American Association for Higher Education. Published bi-monthly. Each issue is devoted to critical topics of interest in higher education, such as academic freedom, autonomy, and faculty and administrations tension.

Chronicle of Higher Education. Washington, D.C.: Chronicle of Higher Education. 46 issues yearly. Following a newspaper format, the *Chronicle* provides excellent coverage of current news about higher education. Regular features include a news summary, including coverage of the status of legislation affecting higher education and news on federal agencies; reviews of new books on higher education; letters to the editor; a gazette of appointments, resignations, deaths, grants and gifts, and coming events; and a list of educational positions available. This publication should be read by everyone who wants to stay up to date about higher education.

Circular Letter. Washington, D.C.: National Association of State Universities and Land-Grant Colleges. 20 issues yearly. Published by the office of the president and known as the "Green Sheet," this publication covers national developments and includes items of special interest from individual universities.

College Administrator and the Courts. Asheville, N.C.: College Administration Publications. Published quarterly. This publication contains briefs of selected higher court cases affecting the administration of colleges and universities.

College Student and the Courts. Asheville, N.C.: College Administration Publications. Published quarterly. This publication contains briefs of selected higher court cases concerning student and institutional relationships.

College Student Journal. Chula Vista, Calif.: Project Innovation. Published quarterly. This publication offers original investigations and theoretical papers that deal with college student values, attitudes, opinions, and learning. It also includes articles on college preparation.

Communique. Washington, D.C.: American Association of University Administrators. Published quarterly. This newsletter focuses on recent court decisions, research notes, and AAUA announcements and activities.

Community and Junior College Journal. Washington, D.C.: American Association of Community and Junior Colleges. Published quarterly. Emphasizing the two-year college, issues of this journal are devoted to programs, teaching efforts, innovations in curriculum, and new approaches to planning and management. The journal also includes how-to articles and discussions on problems, trends, and issues that impinge on the mission of the community college. It is indexed in the fourth issue of each year.

Community College Frontiers. Springfield, Ill.: Sangamon State University and Governors State University. Published quarterly. This journal of analysis, interpretation, and research focuses on the community college. It provides reports on teaching strategies, ideas and opinions on basic education issues, and current analyses of the role of the community college.

Community College Review. Raleigh: North Carolina State University. Published quarterly. This journal features articles on current research, development, issues, programs, and problems particular to community colleges.

Community/Junior College: Quarterly of Research and Practice. Washington, D.C.: Hemisphere. Published quarterly. This journal publishes original research papers in the field of community and junior college education and the social and behavioral sciences. It also contains reviews of various subject areas and recent books.

Compass. Washington, D.C.: Association of Independent Colleges and Schools. Published monthly. This magazine, designed for presidents of private postsecondary business colleges and schools, reprints articles on education from other journals and provides information on legislative changes and funding.

Corporate Giving Profiles. New York: Taft Corporation. Published monthly. This eight-page periodical expands and updates the *Taft Corporate Giving Directory* (see entry number 305). It focuses on the *Fortune* 500 companies responsible for most of America's corporate gifts.

Corporate Giving Watch. New York: Taft Corporation. Published monthly. This newsletter, designed to cover developments in the corporate giving world, provides useful information on individual companies, their executives, and their grant-giving activities. It profiles five to seven individual companies each month.

Current Issues in Higher Education. Washington, D.C.: American Association for Higher Education. 3–4 issues yearly. This publication covers topical issues of importance to higher education. Recent articles include "Strategies for Retrenchment," "Funding Quality Improvement," "Partnerships with Business and the Professions," and "Colleges Enter the Information Society."

Currents. Washington, D.C.: Council for Advancement and Support of Education. Published monthly (except August and December). [Formerly *CASE Currents.*] *Currents* is the only professional periodical devoted exclusively to the concerns of the advancement professional. It covers every functional area of advancement and devotes several issues a year to extensive and in-depth treatment of a major issue in advancement. It also features continuing and new information concerning CASE programs, institutes, and workshops. Special departments include a list of CASE conferences, a "people" section, and "Sound Off," an editorial page giving CASE members and others an opportunity to address controversial issues in advancement.

Editor & Publisher. New York: Editor & Publisher. Published monthly. This periodical covers the latest information about newspapers and is helpful to people who need to keep up with recent information about the newspaper industry in the United States.

Educational Record. Washington, D.C.: American Council on Education. Published quarterly. One of the most respected higher education journals, the *Record* covers a broad range of issues affecting contemporary higher education. A typical table of contents features articles on time management, political models, institutional renewal, and the deanship. It includes a brief book review section.

Educational Researcher. Washington, D.C.: American Educational Research Association. 11 issues yearly. This news and feature magazine offers commentary on events in the field of educational research and articles that synthesize and analyze, in a scholarly fashion, matters of general significance to researchers in education. It includes government news, book reviews, editorials, and research notes.

Effective Speech Writer's Newsletter. Richmond, Va.: Effective Speech Writing Institute, University of Richmond. Published bimonthly. This newsletter offers practical suggestions and current reports on the speech-writing profession. It includes editorials on professional issues, evaluations of writing techniques, interviews, and book reviews.

Enrollment Action Report. Denver, Colo.: Ingersoll Group. Published periodically. This newsletter is designed to assist directors and staff in the admissions field. Typical articles address trends for the future, the recruiting of minorities, marketing to attract graduate students, public relations, leadership and management, management style, planning, publications, communicating with students, and management information systems.

Evaluation Review. Beverly Hills, Calif.: Sage. 6 issues yearly. This publication provides a forum for researchers, planners, and policy makers engaged in developing and implementing studies that address the betterment of the human condition in a variety of institutional and noninstitutional settings. It contains articles on methodological developments and applications of research results, essays, and research briefs.

Federal Register. Washington, D.C.: Office of Federal Register. Published daily (except Saturday and Sunday). The *Federal Register* is a government publication that announces public regulations and legal notices issued by federal agencies. It provides information on proposed as well as final regulations for such pertinent agencies as the Department of Education, the National Science Foundation, and the National Endowment for the Arts.

For Your Information. Washington, D.C.: National Association of State Universities and Land-Grant Colleges. Published monthly. This publication reports on the role of NASULGC member institutions and recent developments in public higher education.

Foundation Giving Watch. New York: Taft Corporation. Published monthly. This periodical covers current trends and important information concerning valuable opportunities in foundation giving.

Foundation Grants Index Bimonthly. New York: Foundation Center. Published periodically. This publication provides current information on foundation giving. Each issue features articles on recent foundation grants and updates on recent changes in foundations in such areas as personnel, requirements, and interests. It also includes lists of grant makers' publications (annual reports, newsletters, and so on), as well as book reviews, notices of courses, seminars, and conferences, and special feature articles on selected issues.

Foundation News: The Magazine of Philanthropy. Washington, D.C.: Council on Foundations. Published bimonthly. This magazine for grant makers and grant seekers provides up-to-date monitoring of the third sector. It features "how-to" articles, essays on philanthropy, case studies, and profiles of successful organizations and people, with regular sections on legislation and regulation, corporate philanthropy, research, community foundations, and book reviews.

Foundation Updates. New York: Taft Corporation. Published monthly. This eight-page periodical provides the latest information on foundations undergoing change or major developments. It follows the same detailed format as *The Taft Foundation Reporter* (see entry number 284).

FRI Monthly Portfolio. Ambler, Pa.: Fund-Raising Institute. Published monthly. Each issue contains a four-page newsletter offering practical notes on new fund-raising techniques and ideas, as well as news on conferences and the activities of nonprofit organizations. It includes updates on fund-raising letter-writing clinics and a detailed practical guide to specific fund-raising activities.

Fund-Raising Management. Garden City, N.Y.: Hoke Communications. Published monthly. This journal for fund-raising professionals contains up-to-date information on developments in legislation, taxes, communications, grant seeking, capital and annual fund-raising campaigns, marketing, and management for nonprofits. It is indexed annually in the December issue.

Fund-Raising Review. New York: American Association of Fund-Raising Counsel. Published bimonthly. This publication summarizes significant articles, speeches, and trends in philanthropy and fund raising.

Giving USA. New York: American Association of Fund-Raising Counsel. Published annually. Most fund raisers consider this compilation of facts and trends on American philanthropy to be essential to their work. The publication reports on total philanthropy in the United States, categorizing giving sources (individuals, bequests, foundations, and corporations) and recipients of contributions (religion, health and hospitals, education, social welfare, arts and humanities, civic and public organizations and others). A valuable feature is its list of some of the leading U.S. private foundations, ranked by amount of grants. Two other sections are of special interest: a chapter on volunteers and an overview written by John J. Schwartz, president of the American Association of Fund-Raising Counsel: "The Changing Climate of Philanthropy."

Grantsmanship Center News. Los Angeles, Calif.: Grantsmanship Center. Published bimonthly. This journal deals with sources of funds, grant writing, grant management, and general management of nonprofit organizations. It includes articles of interest to both grantees and grantors.

Higher Education Abstracts. Claremont, Calif.: Claremont Graduate School. Published quarterly. This publication summarizes current articles, reports, and books about college students, higher education, and student services.

Higher Education and National Affairs. Washington, D.C.: American Council on Education. Published weekly. This publication provides updates on congressional actions in higher education and general news such as presidential appointments, national statistics, and so on.

Journal of Advertising Research. Hanover, Pa.: Advertising Research Foundation. Published bimonthly. This journal features articles of interest to practitioners and users of advertising research.

Journal of College and University Law. Washington, D.C.: National Association of College and University Attorneys. Published quarterly. This journal contains articles and brief commentaries on recent court cases, reviews legislative and administrative developments and current books, and includes an annotated bibliography.

Journal of Higher Education. Columbus: Ohio State University Press and American Association for Higher Education. Published bimonthly. This journal, designed for college and university faculty and administrators, provides ideas, opinions, and reports concerning the implications of current research on higher education. It discusses emerging policy problems and issues, examines existing concepts, and reports on significant case studies applicable in a variety of situations. Typical contents may include articles discussing external degrees, adaptive planning, leadership, and a brief book review section. An annual index is provided in the November/December issue.

Journal of Marketing. Chicago: American Marketing Association. Published quarterly. This journal addresses current theoretical and empirical research. Feature articles include legal developments in marketing, marketing abstracts, book reviews, and editorials.

Journal of Marketing Research. Chicago: American Marketing Association. Published quarterly. This journal publishes research reports on a variety of topics in marketing research, such as buyer behavior, management of market research, sampling and survey methods, strategies, and planning. It also contains recent book reviews.

Journal of Student Financial Aid. Washington, D.C.: National Association of Student Financial Aid Administrators. 3 issues yearly. This publication contains articles on significant issues in student financial aid, such as effective administration, improved delivery, and increased resources.

Journalism Quarterly. Columbia, S.C.: Association for Education in Journalism and Mass Communications. Published quarterly. Devoted to current research in journalism and mass communication, this publication includes features such as research briefs, book reviews, and letters to the editor.

Legislative Review. Denver, Colo.: Education Commission of the States. 20 issues yearly. This publication provides current overviews of state legislative action relating to education.

Liberal Education. Washington, D.C.: Association of American Colleges. Published quarterly. This journal is one of the oldest publications on educational issues. It is devoted to essays that probe and analyze issues of concern to the liberal arts and the sciences and their roles in higher education. The winter issue includes an annual index.

Memo to the President. Washington, D.C.: American Association of State Colleges and Universities. 18 issues yearly. This publication provides news and information about higher education, particularly state colleges and universities. It includes sections on federal relations, international programs, and special reports.

Nonprofit Executive. New York: Taft Corporation. Published monthly. This monthly newsletter is designed specifically for people in nonprofit management. It covers the news and trends of the nonprofit area, contains how-to articles on fund raising, communications, marketing strategies, and organizing volunteers, and offers nonprofit professionals advice on such topics as internal office politics, stress and survival strategies, and nonprofit career paths.

Public Opinion Quarterly. New York: Elsevier Science. Published quarterly. This publication, the journal of the American Association for Public Opinion Research, includes research reports and regular features on current news, book reviews and notes, and polls.

Public Relations Journal. New York: Public Relations Society of America. Published monthly. This publication features an assortment of news items, in-depth articles on critical issues, case histories, and management advice. Its pages typically cover general public relations as well as special applications for public relations firms, business, and nonprofit organizations. Recent issues have included articles on life-style research, salary surveys, producing special events, recent trends in public relations education, television, and institutional body language. In addition to the regular monthly issues, a directory issue is published in September.

Public Relations News. New York: Public Relations News. Published monthly. This publication provides up-to-the-minute information on developments in the practice of public relations, with emphasis on techniques. It also reports on conferences, seminars, and books.

Public Relations Quarterly. Rhinebeck, N.Y.: Public Relations Quarterly. Published quarterly. This is an independent journal for professional public relations practitioners. It provides information on a variety of substantive and practical issues. Past issues have addressed such topics as the relationship of public relations to executive management, licensing, certification, public relations law, and the use of volunteers.

Public Relations Review. New York: Foundation for Public Relations Research and Education. Published quarterly. This is a journal of research and opinion. Primarily devoted to original research, it comments on existing research and needs for future research. While the *Review* is a scholarly journal, it also emphasizes applied research.

Review of Higher Education. Washington, D.C.: Association for the Study of Higher Education. 3 issues yearly. This publication contains theoretical essays, methodological papers, literature reviews, and reports on qualitative and quantitative studies in higher education. Typical contents include review essays on governance books, articles on the politics of higher education, discussions concerning reconciling autonomy and the public interest, and association announcements.

Trends 2000. Washington, D.C.: Association of American Colleges. Published quarterly. This journal summarizes trends in U.S.

colleges and universities. It serves as a guide to planning for institutional development in the 1980s and as a handbook on the role of colleges and universities in the total spectrum of postsecondary education.

Trustee Quarterly. Annandale, Va.: Association of Community College Trustees. Published quarterly. This publication offers articles of interest to community college trustees. It is indexed annually in the spring issue.

Name Index

Names listed in this index are referenced to entry numbers and also to page numbers. Page numbers are given for names that appear in the author's introductions to chapters and sections in the book; they do not duplicate entry numbers. Entry numbers are in boldface type; page numbers are in roman type.

237

Subject Index

Subjects listed in this index are referenced to entry numbers and also to page numbers. Page numbers are given for topics that appear in the author's introductions to chapters and sections in the book; they do not duplicate entry numbers. Entry numbers are in boldface type; page numbers are in roman type.